TULSA'S
HAUNTED MEMORIES

ON THE COVER: The H. R. Johnson Family Cemetery is pictured around 1880.

Tulsa's Haunted Memories

Teri French

ARCADIA
PUBLISHING

Published by Arcadia Publishing
Charleston, South Carolina

Printed in the United States of America

Library of Congress Control Number: 2010924491

For all general information contact Arcadia Publishing at:
Telephone 843-853-2070
Fax 843-853-0044
E-mail sales@arcadiapublishing.com
For customer service and orders:
Toll-Free 1-888-313-2665

Visit us on the Internet at www.arcadiapublishing.com

This book is dedicated to my family and friends.
Your love and support of my strange hobby has been a blessing.
Thank you.

CONTENTS

ACKNOWLEDGMENTS

First I would like to acknowledge the owners of the beautifully preserved historic buildings in Tulsa for working with me and providing me privileged information about these sites. In no particular order, they are Bryce and Sunshine Hill of Tulsa Little Theatre; Peter Mayo of the Brady Theater; Gilcrease Foundation; Linda Collier of the Cave House; Lola, Jennifer, and Drew at Lola's on the Bowery; Janet Gaither and Barbie Raney at the Tulsa Garden Center; the City of Tulsa; Alice Rodgers of Cain's Ballroom; TravelOK; and so many others. It is so important that we keep the history of Tulsa alive for future generations, and your willingness to share and preserve these locations will do that.

My research for this book came from several different sources. I want to thank the principal authors of *Tulsa Spirit* and *Moments in Oklahoma History* for their insight and excellent research materials. Thanks also to the numerous people I interviewed in person and by telephone, who gave me their firsthand accounts and historical information, which was a huge help in putting this project together. A special thanks goes to historian and genealogist Wally Waits, of Muskogee, and to his awesome blogs.

Gratitude goes to my close personal friends who have helped me over the years with their research, friendship, and love. In no particular order, they are Tina Wilson, Karol Olten, Natalie Ford, Mike Buckendorf, Kay Kienzle-Harris, and Ken Hallford; and especially to Kim Lewis for her love, support, and unconditional friendship. A big thank-you also goes out to my very supportive friends and work pals who find my interests amusing and not weird.

A very special acknowledgement goes to the Tulsa Historical Society for use of the pictures from the Beryl Ford Collection. Much appreciation goes to Joshua Peck and our friends at the Tulsa Historical Society and Oklahoma Historical Society.

Of course, I have to thank Ted Gerstle and John Pearson of Arcadia Publishing for giving me this amazing opportunity to share the history and hauntings of Tulsa with the world. Their patience, understanding, and direction have helped me immensely, and I am truly grateful for that. You helped me fulfill an eight-year dream of writing this book.

To my beautiful children—Richie, Brayden, Shayne, and Connor, you are why I breathe.

Lastly, but certainly not least, I am grateful to my lover, partner, and best friend, Russell, who is my biggest advocate and supporter. Your unconditional love still blows me away. And thank you for being my sounding board, dictionary, and thesaurus. You are the best.

All photographs are courtesy of the Beryl Ford Collection, Rotary Club of Tulsa, Tulsa City-County Library, and the Tulsa Historical Society.

FOREWORD

Hauntings and history . . . history and hauntings. At first it seems one would have to be crazy to suggest that these two subjects might be related, but is that necessarily true? Isn't a haunting a story that is passed from person to person? Isn't history a story that is also passed from person to person? Then do these two subjects have more in common than that which is observed superficially? Maybe. Let's take a look at both individually and then view them both as components of human society.

Webster's dictionary defines *haunt* as "to visit or inhabit as a ghost" and "to stay around or persist." Hauntings can incorporate any variety of alleged paranormal phenomena, including ghosts, poltergeists, and demons, but are most often associated with a place perceived to be the dwelling of disembodied spirits and energies of people somehow eternally tied to a particular location. *History* is defined by Webster's as "a branch of knowledge that records and explains past events." To most of us, history involves places, names, and those hard-to-remember dates. From a societal and folkloric perspective, these two subjects are deeply intertwined, as it is almost impossible to have a haunting without an explanation of why it occurs. Explanations are normally historical in nature; in fact, stories of ghosts and ghouls are 99 percent of the time derived from some historical event. Of course, whether one believes in the haunting portion of any history is left to personal doctrine, but one cannot discount the portions of the stories that are historically accurate.

Well that is all well and good, you say to yourself, but Oklahoma is barely 100 years old; there is not much history in this state. Certainly there is not much Western history, when compared to, say, St. Augustine, Florida, a city that can be dated back to 1565 and is linked to Spanish explorer Ponce de Leon's legendary search for the Fountain of Youth . . . or is there?

Oklahoma's European heritage can definitively be dated to 1541, when parts of the state were documented by Spanish explorer Francisco Coronado, who passed through looking for a fabled city of gold. Some scholars claim, however, that a rune stone found in Heavener, Oklahoma, can be assigned to between 600 A.D. and 900 A.D. and was left by Norse explorers claiming a particular piece of land. But this story is a topic of debate among historians. We need to skip forward several hundred years to reach the point when Oklahoma became a big piece of modern history. Prior to the Indian Removal Act of 1830, Oklahoma was known mainly as Indian Territory and was inhabited by a handful of tribes native to the area. These tribes included the Plains Apaches, Arapaho, Caddo, Comanche, Kiowa, Osage, and Wichita tribes. The land itself was thought unfit for settlers, as the ground was rocky in some spots and mainly thick red clay in others. This fact, combined with an unfriendly climate that ran the gamut from blizzards and single-digit temperatures to thunderstorms riddled with huge hailstones and tornadoes—overlaid with a seemingly never-ending wind—made the European Americans feel fine about leaving this area to the native tribes. Because of the lack of Western civilization and its being beyond the influence of law and order, Indian Territory became a favorite hideout of various criminals and outlaws during the 19th and early 20th centuries. Famous rogues such as Jesse James, Belle Starr, and members of the Dalton-Doolin gang made this area their home.

The Indian Removal Act of 1830 was some years in coming to fruition, as it faced severe opposition among some politicians in Washington. So severe were the feelings about this law that some of the military leaders who were assigned the task resigned in disgust. However, the removal operation was in full swing by the latter part of the decade. No one is sure of the number, but records indicate that tens of thousands of native people making up over 60 different tribes were ripped from their homes and forced to march at gunpoint, for over 1,000 miles in some cases. Among the Cherokee tribe alone, over 4,000 men, women, and children died as result of the subhuman conditions of this act. The Cherokee people referred to the move as *Nunna dual Tsuny*, which is literally translated as "the trail where they cried." It became historically known as The Trail of Tears, a name incorporated to cover all the various tribes and all the different trails taken during this period. The U.S. government neglected to tell the seven tribes already living here that they were about to be inundated with new neighbors, who in some cases were sworn lifelong enemies. This led to much bloodshed as the sudden influx of new tribes mixed with those already here. By the mid-19th century, our state had a somewhat strange and violent history.

Skipping ahead to 1889 and the Oklahoma Land Run, we run into yet another influx of people when the U.S. government decided to open the area to settlers. This territory was now known as Oklahoma, a word coined in an 1866 treaty with the Choctaw tribe and derived from the Choctaw language; it means "red people." More conflict arose between the settlers and the tribes living here.

Around the beginning of the 20th century oil was discovered in Oklahoma, which led to many settlements being established only to later dry up as the oil industry crashed and resulting in yet another violent era of our state's history. With the endless influx of people into this area over such a short time, we see the merging of many beliefs and customs.

Author Teri French has assimilated many of these historical events and the stories of the hauntings that go with them in the following pages. She has incorporated her love of history and her love of Green Country and turned out a book rife with history and folklore. Hope you enjoy some of the little-known and, in some cases, creepy stories that she has unearthed in her endeavors!

—Russell White

One

EARLY TULSA

Oklahoma has long been portrayed as flat, dusty land where tumbleweeds roll freely through the deserted streets. Old black-and-white movies depict a territory that was lawless and unruly, where unsuspecting victims were targets of bloodthirsty Indians. It was illustrated as a place where gunslingers did as they pleased and morality did not exist at all.

Long before statehood, early pioneers left their mysteries and mayhem in the streets of Tulsa. Those areas are now populated with homes, businesses, private land, and commercial structures, but at one time they were the sites of bloody battles between Indians, cowboys, soldiers, and other early settlers. From the bitter war between Osage and Creek Indians to the gun-toting cowboys who shot at windows only because the lights were on, from bizarre happenings in the basement of a house on 21st Street to a nickname of "Bloody First Street," Tulsa has its secrets. They include the director and the little girl who still roam the halls of the Tulsa Little Theatre and Bob Wills keeping an eye on the legendary Cain's Ballroom, the bizarre, middle-of-the-night happenings at the beautiful Italianate villa known as the Tulsa Garden Center, and so many other ambiguities that lie within the confines of the beautiful city of Tulsa.

Cowboys, of course, would lend their own colorful mark to the city. The men who worked on nearby ranches would drive large herds of cattle through the streets of Tulsa and terrorize the town. Sounds of gunfire, yelling, and whiskey bottles crashing on the pavement were commonplace. They would shoot above the heads of unsuspecting citizens just to hear them scream. They were even known to nearly cause riots when they shot off their guns in church, threw whiskey bottles, and sang so loudly they would drown out the rest of the congregation. The fellows were always apologetic and paid for the damages generously, so the townspeople would tend to turn their heads from the ruckus. These tales from the past continue to haunt and intrigue both locals and visitors alike. The legends tell of a time long ago, when it truly was the Wild West.

The Tulsa Race Riot of 1921

On one horrifying day in May, Tulsa was the scene of one of the largest and most destructive acts of racial violence in the history of the United States. This infamous event is known as the Tulsa Race Riot. That day is truly a dark moment in Tulsa history, and while it is not a proud one, it is quite significant. Nearly 35 city blocks were destroyed in the segregated area of the Greenwood district, also known as "Black Wall Street." Victims of the race riot were tortured and burned alive in downtown streets for all to see. A disgraced Tulsa remembers the 16-hour riot, and it is still fresh in the memories of its citizens today. The official total of those who perished is 39, but a more accurate estimate by the Red Cross counted over 300 men killed on that fateful day. The horror that Tulsa and the rest of the country witnessed was a devastating example of civil disorder and chaos at its worst. Today there are memorials in the Greenwood district to remind everyone of what was referred to as "the night Tulsa burned." The city has since grown up to own and accept its mistakes, but mass burial sites are still being found today that add to the stain of that incident. Rumors abound that victims of the riot were discarded like old garbage into unmarked graves throughout the city. Some speculated that they were piled high and dumped into water along Riverside Drive. The stories of what happened that day are endless, but all of them freakishly similar. Suspicions of cover-up and conspiracy still linger from the massacre that occurred over 88 years ago.

It all began when a black man named Dick Rowland stepped into an elevator in the Drexel Building operated by a white woman named Sarah Page. A scream was heard and Rowland was witnessed fleeing the scene. There are several rumors that surround the incident, none of which has been proven to be fact. One version is that Rowland and Page were a clandestine couple who had an argument. Another says that Rowland accidentally stepped on Page's foot and tried to catch her as she fell but was spooked by her scream. Somehow those speculations turned ugly and became instigations that Rowland tried to sexually assault Page. Local headlines added fuel to the fire, and the white community talked of lynching. Racial tensions were already high. As police booked Rowland and threw him into lockup, an angry mob was forming. Ready to defend Rowland, the black community surrounded the courthouse where he was being held. These men were armed in an attempt to offer protection to Rowland, but the sheriff denied their request for his release. When an unknown white man tried to disarm a black man, a struggle ensued and caused the firearm to discharge. This sparked the riot. Fighting broke out and continued through the nights of May 31 to June 1. Homes and businesses were looted and burned to the ground. As large, billowing clouds of smoke filled the downtown and Greenwood areas of Tulsa, the mayor asked the governor for assistance, as the police force was too small to contain the rioters. The governor called in the National Guard, who got things under control. As the smoke and flames faded, horrific memories lingered in the streets of downtown Tulsa. It took over 10 years to rebuild after this incident, but it will take much longer for its citizens to forget it. The surviving buildings hold the secrets and sad reminders of those days.

Many famous landmarks in Tulsa that were a part of the chaos are still standing today, and if the walls *could* talk they would leave listeners in awe and disbelief. Tulsa, also known as Tulsey Town, has a very rich history that will both stun and excite you.

Men gather outside Tulsa's Convention Hall (Brady Theater) as victims are corralled into the building. The theater was said to be a safe place for victims of the race riots, but this picture shows they are at gunpoint with their hands in the air. Once they were inside, no one knows exactly what happened, but rumors claim that torture went on.

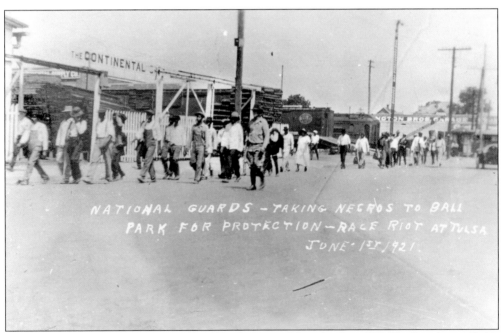

Men are being taken to McNulty Park Ball Field by the National Guard in June 1921. The Guard was called in during the escalating race riots to bring order and peace. The ball field was said to be a place men were taken to protect them from rioters.

Men are causing disturbances outside the Convention Hall during the Tulsa Race Riots of 1921. Though held at gunpoint with arms in the air, victims of the riot were claimed to be taken to Convention Hall as a safety precaution until the riot was under control.

Men gather outside the Brady Theater in response to the venue becoming a holding cell for victims of the race riots. Once the doors were locked, no one knows what happened inside. Rumors relate some rather gruesome details.

National Guardsmen lead riot victims to McNulty Park for safekeeping in June 1921.

Victims of the race riot are herded like cattle into the Brady Theater in June 1921. The men are being held at gunpoint and searched as they enter the theater, which was falsely promised to be a safe haven for them.

Armed men ride around in a car looking for targets during the Tulsa Race Riot of 1921. Men took the law into their own hands until the National Guard was called to come in and restore order.

Wagons and men gather in Greenwood to pick up bodies of the race riot victims all around the downtown area. Rumors claim the men involved with the riot wanted to dispose of the bodies quickly before the Red Cross could do an actual count. It is said that bodies were piled on these wagons like old trash and discarded at various places around the city.

15

A body lies in the middle of the street in downtown Tulsa after the 1921 Tulsa Race Riot. The man was lynched, hanged by the wire lying behind him. He was pulled down and placed on the street until his body was picked up by the National Guard. The victim's name is not known.

Tulsa Outlaws

Along with its share of cowboys, Tulsa had its fair share of outlaws as well. The town was widely known as a rendezvous for outlaw gangs. In 1915, Kate "Ma" Barker offered a hideout to her outlaw son Doc Barker in the two-room shack she rented at 401 North Cincinnati Avenue. In 1918, Doc Barker stole a government car during the Fourth of July celebration and killed a night watchman at St. John's Hospital. In 1928, George "Machine Gun" Kelly was arrested for vagrancy and bootlegging and spent some time in a Tulsa jail. He was later convicted for kidnapping oilman Charles Urshel. In the 1930s, Bonnie Parker and Clyde Barrow often passed through Tulsa on their crime sprees. In 1932, Charles "Pretty Boy" Floyd sought refuge in his hideout at 512 East Young Street. Though 20 lawmen surrounded the house, Floyd still managed to escape out the back door. After they became outlaws, the Dalton brothers attended church in late 1889 at the First United Methodist Church, known as the little white church on North Main Street. There was a sort of gentleman's agreement that in exchange for immunity, the town would furnish an asylum. Those famous outlaws and the pandemonium they brought with them are yet another reason Tulsa has so many haunted memories.

The Wild, Wild West

As the free-range way of life came to a halt, the Old West faded and Tulsa soon became known as the Oil Capital of the World. The discovery of oil drew many to the city, and some of the more prominent characters had their secret agendas. Those men brought not only insight and determination to Tulsa but also a Zionist following, bootlegging, private clubs, and secret societies. Prestige and social status came with a price that has left its currency throughout the city.

At one time, brothels lined the streets downtown. Prostitutes, rowdiness, and poker games frequently ended in arguments and shoot-outs. On New Year's Day 1909, the *Tulsa World* reported on an escapade involving two highwaymen who caused a major traffic jam in Tulsa. The three handkerchief-masked bandits robbed 25 men on the public roads and took cash, watches, rings, and even a pair of horses. Despite Prohibition, a whiskey-induced rampage caused many such incidents. Tulsans insisted on having their whiskey, and would do just about anything to keep it. Those days are long gone, but they most certainly left ghostly impressions on Tulsa.

While it is true that lawlessness, uprising, and inhumane treatment were once a part of Tulsa's past, that place of turmoil has evolved and been named America's Most Beautiful City, where citizens are some of the most caring and giving people anywhere. The past 100 years of haunted history are written in the walls of historic landmarks that stand majestically throughout the city. It is no secret that the birth of Oklahoma was a painful one. Tulsa has its regrets, but it is also a

This is one of the many spooky, older Tulsa buildings that stir up memories of haunts and strange happenings.

city that has triumphed over devastation and defeat to become a place of beauty and a community that many are proud to call home.

Throughout the city of Tulsa lies a haunted past. Some of the more obscure areas in the city with a very interesting story to tell are detailed in the following pages.

The Hanging Tree

Sitting stately and quiet among the Oktoberfest headquarters at Three North Lawton Avenue is a magnificent 216-year-old Burr oak known as The Hanging Tree. A short rope, a noose, and a large branch were how society dealt with those who violated Creek Indian law in the late 1800s. The eerie lower limb is 12 feet from the ground and makes it easy to picture a convicted man standing on a wagon with a rope around his neck as the wagon slowly moves from under his feet. Between 15 and 20 people were reportedly hanged from the tree between 1870 and 1889. Most notable were three cattle rustlers who were all hanged at the same time.

In the 1920s, as the land was being developed, workers digging for sewer lines unearthed many human remains at the base of the hanging tree. Whether or not they were the bones of the three cattle rustlers or other outlaws who were sentenced to hang, they certainly supported the legends that surround the tree. It was never found out whose bones they were or whatever happened to them, but Tulsans were startled at the discovery. Houses and duplexes were built along the area and all the while, the historic tree stood grandly in the neighborhood as a witness to past. In 1977, a man named Albert Freiberg owned the site. Freiberg lived there and asked the Oklahoma state forestry division to take samples from the tree to determine its age. These samples proved the tree to be over 185 years old at that time. Later Monte Troxell purchased the land for $29,000 and a promise—to never remove the old tree. Troxell kept that promise and tore down everything in the area except the tree. In 1989, the tract was the proposed site for a new criminal justice center, but Tulsa citizens feared the historic tree would be removed, and a petition was formed. The citizens won, and the tree still stands today.

It is said that Burr oak trees usually do not get as large or live as long as the Hanging Tree. It is unknown how the tree has endured as it has, but there is reputedly a spring underneath that has helped in its growth. Legends say that on certain nights, the distinct squeaking sound of an old rope twisting in the breeze can be heard.

Bloody First Street

Right alongside the newly constructed 19,199-seat BOK (Bank of Oklahoma) Center is First Street in downtown Tulsa. It was said that on Saturday nights, when oilmen had money in their pocket, whisky on their breath, and too much time on their hands, they would ride along First Street terrorizing the neighborhood with screams and gunfire. If a light were left on in a window of a house, drunken cowboys would shoot at it for mere fun. Anarchy was the theme back then. Murders, fights, and knifings became so frequent that the street was given the nickname "Bloody First Street." It was not uncommon to find dead men lying in the street who bled to death from a fight the night before. In fact, a 12-year-old boy witnessed this firsthand. As he left his house early one morning to run his paper route, he found a man lying bloody in his front yard. Apparently, the man had been stabbed in a fight and staggered along the street to eventually collapse in the boy's front yard, bleeding to death—an example of just how First Street became "Bloody First Street."

Dead Man's Curb

Less than a mile from Bloody First Street is Dead Man's Curb at the corner of Second Street and Frisco Avenue in downtown Tulsa. This was once the site of Tulsa's first graveyard. The cemetery was established over 125 years ago and covered over an acre of land. Bodies were interred here from 1882 until 1905, and it is said to hold Creek Indians and early pioneers. Some of the more notable people buried in Tulsa's first graveyard were "Tulsa Jack" Yockey, a train robber who was shot to death during a dispute in 1894. Early merchant Jeff Archer was also buried there. His prominent family has a street named after it in downtown Tulsa.

In 1905, the city paid contractors to move the bodies and named Oaklawn Cemetery at 11th Street and Peoria Avenue the city's official graveyard. Bodies in the original graveyard at Dead Man's Curb were excavated and moved. Many were transferred to the new cemetery, but others were not so fortunate. Numerous unmarked graves were not touched until city workers bulldozed the area to make way for street construction in the 1920s. Being around the Second and Frisco area became a bit unnerving as the discovery of bodies and bones continued to be a frequent occurrence. A homeowner who lived in the area discovered human bones on his property in 1934, and years earlier a mummified mother and child were found in the area as well. The homeowner tried to get the city to take ownership of the bones but got no response. He eventually made a grave for them in his backyard. In 1948, six more corpses were found when workers were digging a basement.

Discoveries of bodies continued in 1955, 1967, and 1970 when backhoes were digging for construction. More recently, bones of adolescent boys were found in the area in both 1995 and 2005. And as recently as 2007, the new BOK arena was breaking ground, and, as before, more bodies were found. Is it any wonder, with so many deficient resting places, that Tulsa would be home to many ghosts?

George W. Mowbray was Tulsa's first undertaker.

Looking north on *Third Street* in downtown Tulsa, this image shows the young city in 1896.

Revitalization is going on in downtown Tulsa, and it is likely that as progress continues more bodies and bones will be found. It prompts the question of how much of downtown Tulsa was used as a burial ground. Is this the reason for the restless spirits that roam in the streets, businesses, and homes? It surely can be a contributing factor to the ghostly stories and sightings.

Cherry Street

Cherry Street was constructed in the early 1900s, when horse-drawn buggies and trolley cars were the main sources of transportation. For a time, it was renamed 15th Street, but later changed back to Cherry Street. The name Cherry Street can be found on the original plat maps that date back prior to statehood. Due to consistent spectral activities that have occurred along the corridor, 15th Street earned a reputation and the nickname "Area Fifteen." Today Cherry Street is a narrow, tree-lined four-lane avenue that boasts large mansions and structures that have since been renovated for commercial use. Along Cherry Street lie trendy restaurants, bookstores, bars, antique dealers, retail clothing stores, and specialty shops. The entire area is a famous landmark in Tulsa and is listed on the National Register of Historic Places. Some even say the name Cherry Street derived from the fact that the street was once a very popular area for prostitutes and brothels. Originally this area was outside the city limits and had no bathroom facilities or running water. Trolley tracks in the streets have since been paved over, but at one time horses stood tied up along the dusty streets in front of trading posts and saloons. It is yet another area of Tulsa holding some ghostly secrets.

Peace of Mind Bookstore

On Cherry Street is a New Age bookstore and gift shop called Peace of Mind. It occupies an old two-story structure that was a hotel in the early 1900s. There is a bookstore on the second floor, and gifts and novelties downstairs as well as a bar next door. The old building was said to have been a brothel that was kept intentionally separated from the business district so occupants could better get away with bootlegging and roundups. Employees of the bookstore have some rather strange stories relating to ghostly activity. The bookstore itself is somewhat unusual and sells books on witchcraft, demonology, world religions, theology, philosophy, and things that are otherworldly. Customers get the feeling they are being watched and many patrons claim the place gives them a creepy feeling, especially upstairs where the books are sold. An undeniable energy surrounds anyone who enters the store. Employees have reported some very strange things happening inside the bookstore and a ghostly presence that seems to lend a specific energy to the place.

Tulsa's Haunted Memories

Could it be the collection of books on witchcraft, demonology, and the supernatural that make this place uncomfortable for some? Or could these things be bringing out the restless spirits already there? Whatever it is, some are convinced the place is haunted. Workers at the shop have reported ghostly apparitions, books being placed in areas they should not be, items being moved, doors slamming, and gifts flying off shelves as if they were being hit with some force. Whatever "force" is there, it has no trouble letting the employees know about its presence and making sure that it is not soon forgotten.

Hardware stores, trading posts, saloons, and general stores begin to mark the landscape of early Tulsa in this c. 1890 image.

In the beginning, Tulsa had dry goods stores, a post office, and saloons.

Early Tulsa shows signs of growth, as stores and trading posts line the area that will later become Main Street, looking northward from Fourth Street downtown.

TULSA - POPULATION 200
MAIN ST., LOOKING SOUTH
YEAR 1889

In Tulsa's early days, before "Black Wall Street," herds of cattle often milled in the street as men tied up their horses at their favorite watering holes.

Looking south on Main Street, this 1892 image shows Thomas Jefferson Archer's second Tulsa store building, located south of the Frisco Railroad right-of-way on the east side of Main Street. Archer is in the center of the picture, standing on the porch.

Tulsa's Haunted Memories

Old Mansions and Homes on Cherry Street and the Old Funeral Home

There are several old mansions along Cherry Street that were once homes to oilmen who found wealth in Tulsa. Today many have been renovated into offices. One particular house is consistently up for lease. An attorney who leased that building for a time refuses to ever have an office in a haunted location again. Very strange things have happened in that home. The lead attorney was working late one evening when a strong male voice yelled at him, "Get Out!" It startled him, and he indeed left the building and would not work there at night again. Other workers at the office confirmed that machines would turn off and on by themselves, their children would claim to see other children that were not there, and they heard startling loud noises. During the law firm's stay in the building files would often go missing, only to turn up later in strange areas where they should not have been.

A prior owner of the house recalls hiring a plumber for some maintenance. The plumber went into the basement to check the water tank. A short time passed before the plumber came running up the stairs and told the owner that he would not go down there again. When asked why, the plumber said there were children running around bothering him and tugging at his legs. The plumber was so disturbed by the incident that he left his tool box in the basement and refused to go down and retrieve it. He never returned to the house after that.

A former employee of the law firm said that the same thing happened to her daughter. She brought her daughter to work with her one day and set her in a vacant office to keep her occupied, but the daughter came back into her mother's office visibly shaken and disturbed. She claimed that children were running around her, taunting and laughing at her, and tugging at her legs. She said they were playing with the phone cord and making odd noises. The daughter had not heard the stories of the house before and refused to go back to her mother's office with her ever again. The firm's employees experienced many other strange incidents. Soda cans would be knocked over seemingly on their own, ruining keyboards and causing a mess. They also frequently found a puddle of water that would mysteriously appear in the upstairs hallway with no water source nearby. Office doors would shut and lock on their own, trapping those working inside until someone came to their rescue. The head attorney once noticed someone peering into his car in the parking lot and went down to see who it was but the woman had disappeared. He later saw her dragging something across the back yard when he went to take the trash outside. Another person with him did not see the woman when he asked her what the lady was doing.

An old man who lived next door his entire life told the employees of the law office of a time when the house was occupied by a sick, deranged individual who was convicted of murder. The story says he would torture and torment his victims before killing them and burying them in the back yard. The neighbor claimed a book was written about the murders and the man was eventually caught. The bodies dug up from the back yard guaranteed him a life sentence in prison. While the employees had trouble finding information on this case, they had no doubt that something bad had happened inside the home due to their experiences inside. Cold spots, footsteps, the feeling of being watched, and the sounds of doors slamming when a worker was alone inside the house were so frequent they caused the workers to question their own sanity.

It eventually became so bothersome the firm moved out of the building. While it remains unclear why the structure is haunted, its history is nothing short of disquieting. The house was once a funeral home, and the owners were arrested for some shady dealings. It seems they would talk grieving families into allowing them to file their insurance claims. When those families did not receive any money and efforts to retrieve it were unsuccessful, they called the police. Tulsa police decided to pay a visit to the funeral home and ask some questions, but what they found inside was alarming and disgusting. In the kitchen of the home, lying out in the open, were torsos and limbs of the deceased. They also found caskets full of body parts from different people. The owners of the funeral home had told families they were unable to have an open casket showing, but it was found out that the reason they did this was to save money by fitting several bodies into one casket. To have opened the casket during the funeral would have revealed the fraud. The police were disgusted by the lack of empathy and care given by the funeral home owners but were hampered since there were no laws protecting the dead. It was not murder; the people who were dismembered were already dead. The best authorities could do was charge the funeral home owners with insurance and mail fraud. The husband and wife were sentenced to prison. The wife was released in 2005, but the husband is still doing time in an Oklahoma City prison.

The Little White Church

In north Tulsa, there is an ominous little white church that has some stories to tell. The church is supposed to have been established in 1917, but legend says the Dalton Brothers gang attended services there after they became outlaws in 1889. It seems the church had an understanding with the Daltons. It was noted they would escape through the basement after services to keep from getting caught. They could worship without fear of alerting the authorities if they were truly repentant for their sins.

The basement the Daltons used as an escape route was built to accommodate a Sunday school started by E. A. Robinson. This cellar also acted as the main church, but as the congregation grew, the basement was unable to handle the capacity. A new, more permanent place of worship was in order. It was built over the basement, which would later become a gym and fellowship hall. That structure still stands today and has become a landmark for drivers on I-244.

TULSA'S HAUNTED MEMORIES

In the 1940s and after World War II, residents of Tulsa began to move south of town to the growing neighborhoods springing up there. The neighborhood surrounding the church eventually began to house low-income and lower-middle-class families. An area of wealth and prosperity had now become an area of poverty. It was around 1950 that a huge split of the congregation was initiated by racial hatred and disdain. The church admitted black families, much to the discomfort of its current members, many of whom left. In 1969, a daycare was started in the church with seven children, four paid workers, and two volunteers. About a decade later Emergency Infant Services occupied the building to aid low-income and poverty-stricken mothers and children in need of everyday necessities. The office operated out of the location for 14 years and then moved to a location in downtown Tulsa. By the mid-1980s, the little white church was dilapidating quickly and water damage caused the need to remove the steeple. Shortly after that and just before church services one Sunday morning, the ceiling of the chapel came crashing down. Luckily, no one was inside at the time, but Sunday school services were going on in the basement. The church was then disbanded, but some continued to worship in the old building after repairs were made.

During the time the daycare occupied the building, around 6:00 one morning a teacher opening the center became alarmed when she heard the sounds of a child crying. Fearing a child had been left overnight, the woman frantically searched the building, which turned up empty. This happened a few more times and as people traced the child's voice, they realized it was coming from the kitchen. They soon realized the crying had started around the same time a refrigerator was donated by a local family. When contacted and asked about the refrigerator, family members disclosed they could not have the appliance in their home, as it was a reminder of the most horrible day of their lives. One of their children, while playing hide and seek, got into the refrigerator and was locked inside. The family eventually found the child but he had already perished from lack of oxygen.

There were not only sounds of a child in the kitchen but sightings of one as well. A former cook reported being visited repeatedly by a little girl. The director dismissed the reports, telling the cook there were "no such things as ghosts." Just as the director announced her opinion, one of her certificates hanging on the wall went crashing to the floor, sending broken glass all over her office.

One evening, as workers were closing down the center for the day, a distinct sound of footsteps was heard. When one of the workers asked for whoever it was to identify himself, a loud bang startled everyone. Security was called in, but a thorough sweep of the building found no one and no explanation for the loud noise. Even more odd, the second floor where the noise emanated from was locked up and secure.

The daughter of one member of the church congregation recalls getting locked into a closet in the Fellowship Hall. Her frightened calls alerted two children who came to her rescue and opened the door, which, disturbingly, had no lock. A pew was placed in front of the closet and none of the children would go near it after that.

Indeed, the Little White Church has an eerie aura to it. Reports of growling noises in the sanctuary and apparitions walking through the gym became commonplace. Children in gym clothing would be seen walking towards the north side of the building and up the stairs only to vanish. Following these visits, a door that was normally locked would always be found unlocked. Children have complained of feelings of being watched in the very cold back stairwell and have reported seeing an old man staring at them from the balcony above. Lights have been reported to go on and off in locked rooms, and a female soprano has been heard singing and walking down the hallway. It seems that the past is still alive and well in the Little White Church, where the congregations of days past still visit.

Two

TULSA HOMES
AND MANSIONS

The Tulsa Garden Center

One of the most breathtaking places in Tulsa is the Tulsa Garden Center. The beautiful Italianate villa was designed by noted Tulsa architect Nobel Flemming. Construction on the 21 room, 10 bathroom home began in 1919, and was completed in 1921 at a cost of more than $100,000. David Travis built the house and his brother, Samuel, lived next door in a home that he built, which is now the headquarters for the Tulsa Historical Society. David Travis was a Russian immigrant whose original name was Rabinowitz. He moved to Tulsa in 1913 with his family and earned his wealth in the oil field equipment salvage business.

The ballroom on the lower level of the mansion was the location for Jewish services during the time the Travis family was in residence. The cobblestone driveway was laid by hand when David and his brother ran out of money to complete it. The arboretum parking lot was once the site of a swimming pool with adjacent tennis courts. The ceiling in the original library is gold leaf, and the stained glass ceiling over the open stairway was originally a skylight.

Arthur Hull bought the house in 1923, at which time he added the Lord and Burnham conservatory and sunken gardens. Arthur's wife, Mary, died suddenly from an illness shortly after moving into the house, and the Great Depression soon ravaged the nation. The house was put on the market for a mere $25,000 but had no takers.

Finally, in 1934, George Snedden purchased the distressed mansion, and his family remained in the home until 1949. W. G. Skelly bought the property in 1950 for his daughter, but neither of them lived there. Skelly eventually sold the historic mansion to the city of Tulsa as an education resource center and meeting place for horticultural organizations.

Since that time, the villa has been home to more than just garden clubs. Wandering the halls of the Garden Center, a visitor never knows who or what they might encounter. How could a place of such beauty house ghostly specters? Some say a distraught Mary still lingers in the dream house she could not enjoy due to her untimely death. Others say it is her niece Roberta Jane Stewart, who used to frequently visit Mary and Arthur after they moved in. It is said that Roberta would "go a little crazy," acting as if she was the lady of the house. She would get delusional thoughts of being the owner of the grand mansion, and it seems those delusions are still present today. The phantom footsteps heard throughout the mansion are believed to be Roberta claiming her stake.

When Mary died in 1931, her body lay in state in the south solarium for viewing. To this day that room, which faces the sun on the south side of the house and is full of windows, is cooler than any other room in the home. There is a definite chill that permeates the area.

A former caretaker of the mansion recounts hearing running footsteps on the second floor landing each morning when he opened, but thorough searches never turned up a living soul. Thinking that his employer was testing him, the caretaker finally asked several questions. He wanted to know why every morning he found the attic door unlocked after locking it at night. The library lights would go on as he stepped into his car in the parking lot, yet the lights would be off the next morning. Decorative bulbs in the wall sconces would explode for no apparent reason, and lights would suddenly not work after having been functional minutes earlier. The wiring was inspected and passed all tests. Sounds of footsteps on the clay roof tiles above the third floor servants' quarters caused workers to refuse to enter the area without an escort. Many employees also claimed to hear footsteps close behind them, only to turn around and find they were alone. One Halloween night, the alarm company called the caretaker to the house. When he and the police arrived they found all the doors wide open on the front side of the house, yet nothing had been disturbed or taken.

During events at the house, strange things have been said to happen. One time, as a group entered the building, the elevator by the front door dinged, opened, and seemingly operated on its own. Simultaneously, the doorbell began to ring incessantly and the telephone rang off the hook. All of these occurrences at the same time caused some excitement among the group. The door was made of glass, and the patrons could see no one on the opposite side ringing the doorbell. When the phone was answered, there was nothing on the line but static. The elevator made a few more rounds before coming to a stop on the first floor. Never before had the employees seen the house go so crazy with no reasonable explanation. They say that it has not happened again.

Shadowy figures have been seen in the ballroom and upper elevator areas of the home, and people have been touched by an unseen entity. Employees would arrive at the house upon opening for business to find furniture rearranged upstairs in the elevator sitting room. They would find doors to offices standing wide open and unlocked when no one had been in the home. Disembodied voices have been heard throughout the old mansion, and papers have been witnessed moving across a room to assemble into a neat pile on the floor. The Garden Center is a place of past wealth and prestige, but it is also the home to some pesky ghosts who make their presence quite known in the most obvious ways.

The Thomas Gilcrease Home

The Thomas Gilcrease house is known as one of the most haunted homes in Tulsa. While the home's history is not one of tragedy or disaster, sightings and firsthand accounts of ghostly activity are so frequent they permeate the grounds and facilities of the Gilcrease property.

Thomas Gilcrease was born in Louisiana in 1890, but due to his mother's Creek Indian heritage, the family moved to Indian Territory when Thomas was just an infant. In 1906, at age 16, Thomas sued the tribal government for membership and won. This lawsuit allotted him 160 acres of land in Glenpool, Oklahoma. The land later turned out to include some of the largest oil fields in the state. In 1908, Gilcrease married Belle Harlow, an Osage tribe member. They would divorce after 14 years, but not before they had two sons, Thomas Jr. and Barton Eugene.

In 1911, when Thomas reached the age of 21, he had acquired great wealth and traveled the world. He opened Gilcrease Oil in San Antonio, Texas, and also maintained an office in Europe. While in Europe, he visited museums and took a particular interest in Native American art. Since it was not a hot commodity at that time, he began to collect it and amassed the largest private collection of Native American art in the world.

It was a beautiful fall day in 1913 when Gilcrease was driving along and noticed a big two-story house being erected in the hills on the west side of Tulsa. The house was being constructed with materials that came directly from the hills that surrounded it, and this impressed Gilcrease. Prominent Tulsa attorney Flowers Nelson was building the home for his fiancée, Kerri, so they would have a place to live after they wed. Due to some unfortunate circumstances, Kerri died a sudden, tragic death during the construction of their home, and Nelson could not bear to live there without her. Gilcrease loved the native sandstone materials that were used on the exterior of the home, so he walked up and made an offer to Nelson.

On December 26, 1913, Thomas Gilcrease purchased the house, and it became his private residence, also known as Tom's Place or The House on the Hill. After his divorce from Belle Harlow in 1922, Gilcrease again traveled the world and rented out the house. At one time he attempted to sell it, but the loan went into default, and Thomas bought the house back.

In 1928 Gilcrease married Norma Smallwood, Tulsa's very first Miss America, who was only 19 at the time. They had one child, a daughter named Des Cygne, but they were only married for five short years before they divorced. It is said that Norma moved her mother into the house with them and that she was a social butterfly and loved to have big, lavish parties. Thomas was a private person and did not like all the commotion in his house. He and Norma fought continuously about the frequent parties, and it is rumored that this was the reason for their divorce. On the divorce petition, Gilcrease cites extreme cruelty and neglect of duty by Norma as the basis for the dissolution of their marriage.

In 1943, Thomas Gilcrease was living in San Antonio, Texas, and opened an orphanage in the Tulsa house for underprivileged children of the Five Civilized Tribes. His brother and sister-in-law ran the coed orphanage. Girls slept on the second floor, and boys stayed in another area of the property, separate from the girls. Due to a decline in oil prices, Thomas was unable to continue to fund the orphanage, which had to close down by 1949. The decline in oil revenue threw Gilcrease into debt to the tune of $2.5 million. This was an enormous sum of money in the 1940s. The citizens of Tulsa so feared that Gilcrease would leave the city and take his massive art collection with him that they raised a private bond that passed 3 to 1. The city of Tulsa paid off Gilcrease's debt, and in turn he deeded the collection to the city, which is still home to the Gilcrease Museum. The Gilcrease house became his exclusive residence from 1949 to 1962, when he suffered a heart attack inside his home and died. He is buried along with his parents in a tomb on the property.

While this may not sound like a history that would lead to a haunting, it is quite evident that Thomas Gilcrease is still keeping a careful eye on his property. Firsthand accounts of strange activity at the home and museum make it undeniable. Sightings of Gilcrease's ghosts happen so often they result in a very high turnover rate of night watchmen.

A grand foyer with winding stairs and great rooms on either side greets visitors entering the front door of the Gilcrease house. Those great rooms both have fireplaces and hardwood floors that connect to other rooms and complete the downstairs floor plan of the home. On the south side of the foyer are a living area, formal dining room, breakfast nook, and kitchen, which connects to a butler's pantry. Part of this section was once Gilcrease's private suite. The stairwell winds around to the upper portion of the home, where there is a long hallway with several closets, a bathroom, and three bedrooms. Upstairs also has a veranda with a beautiful view of downtown Tulsa and the east side of the Gilcrease hills. There is also a small hobby room with a very low ceiling that has several windows and offers a gorgeous panoramic view of the hills to the west side of the property. The house is quite stunning and, if the walls could talk, they would most likely leave listeners stunned.

Built by Flowers Nelson in 1913, this home was purchased by Thomas Gilcrease the day after Christmas. Made of sandstone that came directly from the Gilcrease Hills, the mansion is said to be one of the most haunted in Tulsa. This image dates from 1915..

TULSA'S HAUNTED MEMORIES

The Gilcrease house used to be the home of the Tulsa Historical Society, and former curator Dan McPike recalls a chilling incident that happened to him one evening. He was closing up the house for the night, turning off lights, closing doors, and getting ready to head out when he stopped dead in his tracks in the foyer. He was standing by the front door when he noticed something on the stairs. He turned to see the ghost of Thomas Gilcrease standing at the bend of the stairs. Gilcrease looked at him, nodded his head, and went upstairs. McPike stood there in disbelief, and as quickly as the ghostly presence came, so did it vanish.

One balmy summer evening, museum night guards were alerted to a motion alarm that went off inside the Gilcrease home that sits adjacent to the museum. The motion sensor in the south upstairs bedroom had been tripped. Fearing someone had broken into the house, the guards called the Tulsa police to investigate. When the police arrived, they brought along a trained police dog and went into the house to find the intruder. As they approached the stairs, the dog started to cower, growl, and whimper, and it refused to go up the stairs. The dog then turned around and bolted toward the front door in a determined effort to leave the house. This was a trained police dog! The officer realized the dog would be of no help to him and went upstairs with his gun drawn only to return empty handed. The officer could not find a reason for the false alarm nor did he find what spooked the dog right out of the house.

Another ghostly presence at the Gilcrease estate is that of a phantom cat. Visitors have reported hearing the very distinct sound of a cat meowing but have been unable to find a cat in sight. Those peeking through the front door window from outside have witnessed a nearly transparent feline running through the foyer area. It seems that Gilcrease's cat liked the house so much that it chose not to leave, either.

However, the employees of the museum are a testament to the truly unusual things that go on at the Gilcrease. A man named Jim had just moved to Tulsa from Minnesota. He was working on getting an education in law enforcement and applied for a job at the Gilcrease museum until he finished his studies. As usual, there was an opening for a night watchman, and Jim got the job. On his first night at work, he was patrolling the hallways of the museum and doing his rounds when he noticed a man in a bowler hat and suit looking at a painting. Since the hours of operation had long passed and the doors were locked, Jim, with one had on his weapon, approached the stranger. He came up behind the man and made a demand for his name and his reason for being in the museum. The man turned around, looked at Jim, and said, "This is a Remington painting. In all of Remington's paintings, he hides a rabbit. Can you find the rabbit?" Jim was shocked at the intruder's lack of concern and again asked for the man's name, but he only repeated himself, saying, "Can you find the rabbit?" Jim then looked away from the man to search for the rabbit in a momentary lapse of reason, and when he turned around, the man was gone. Jim removed his radio from his lapel and called to the guards at the front desk who were watching on security

This yoke was once used for cattle or oxen to pull wagons. In this photograph, it is being used as decoration on a private cattle gate in Tulsa. Many refer to it as a reminder of the gallows that were once all over the city.

cameras. He told his co-workers of his find and how the man was gone and loose in the museum. The guards told him they had watched him on the cameras talking to himself but did not see anyone with him. As the other men teased him for being the "new, weird guy," Jim was getting irritated and began to frantically look around the museum for the man. He asked the other guards to keep an eye on the cameras. He was told the cameras were clear and that no one unauthorized was in the museum, but Jim was not convinced. He had just talked to a man, and he knew he had to be somewhere in the building. For the remainder of the evening, Jim looked in every hallway, room, bathroom, closet, nook, and cranny but did not see the man for the rest of the night. He was baffled. When his shift was over, he had to write a report on his experience. While he was describing the man he had seen, a supervisor told him to stop writing and follow him. Jim followed the supervisor into a back room where there was a portrait hanging on the wall. The supervisor pointed at the portrait and asked if this was the man he had seen. Jim confirmed that was the man he was talking to, and the supervisor told him that was Mr. Gilcrease, whom the museum had been named after. Jim, with a sigh of relief, asked the supervisor why Mr. Gilcrease refused to reveal his identity and was surprised to learn that Gilcrease had died some 20 years earlier. Jim said that was his first experience with a ghost.

Another truly fascinating story from the Gilcrease involves a beautiful display of fragile artifacts that were on display in the museum. Coordinators carefully placed the delicate pieces on a glass shelf and roped it off. The day after setting up the display, museum workers noticed that one of the pieces from the top shelf was missing. They found it on the floor, neatly pushed back and tucked under the bottom shelf. This seemed impossible. If that artifact had fallen off the top shelf it would have shattered into many pieces. Thinking nothing of it, the workers put the piece back on the top self of the display and went about their business. When they returned to work the next day, the same piece was missing and was once again found on the floor, neatly tucked under the bottom shelf. This went on for a few days and prompted curators to research the artifacts a bit more. What they found was startling. The piece that had been removed did not belong with that collection. They removed the piece, and the display was never tampered with again. It's most certain that Thomas Gilcrease is still very particular on how things are displayed at his museum.

The museum gift shop is not exempt from ghostly encounters, either. Employees have witnessed the radio mysteriously turning off and on by itself. They have even gone so far as to replace the radio, but the problem persists. When they close the gift shop at night and begin to exit, the radio will suddenly come on. Someone will go in, turn the radio off, and again head for the exit only to hear the sounds of music coming from the radio. Many times, the radio has remained on all night because of someone's refusal for it to be turned off. Gilcrease did like music, and so it is believed that he is the one tampering with the radio.

The Gilcrease has long had an eerie reputation, and many other strange things have been reported. Not only have visions of Gilcrease himself been noted, but visitors and employees alike have made claims of seeing the lights turn on and off in the house when no one is inside. There have also been sightings of a silhouette peering out the windows of the upper floors. A woman's voice has been heard inside the house, which some believe could be the beloved Kerri, who never got to live in her home. Children are said to be seen and sensed inside the home that was once an orphanage, and toys have been placed and misplaced around the house. Could it be the children who were helped by the orphanage? It was such a place of solitude and comfort for those children that it could very well be where they choose to spend eternity. Whoever is there, it is not difficult to believe with all the direct accounts that the Gilcrease is one of the most haunted places in Tulsa.

The Cave House

At 1623 West Charles Page Boulevard stands a 1,520-square-foot oddity known as the Cave House, Flintstone House, the Hill House, The Cave, the Castle, or simply the Weird House. The odd-looking structure with many names has been a staple in Tulsa since the early 1900s. The Cave House was built in the 1920s by Joseph Koberling as a restaurant appropriately named The Cave Garden. It was well known for its fried chicken and apple pies but was notorious for being a speakeasy at night. It once had a secret dining room and bar where patrons could purchase liquor during Prohibition. Even the likes of Pretty Boy Floyd were known to frequent the restaurant because of its hidden rooms and underground tunnels for easy and silent escapes.

Its name derives from the fact that it was built into a hillside. Deep within that hill is where the secret dining room and tunnels are said to exist. Rumors claim that hidden spaces were sealed off after a huge bust in the late 1920s. Legend says that behind the current fireplace are the hallway, stairs, and hidden rooms that lead to a magical ballroom. This has all been sealed up, though current owners have considered excavating the area to see if the tales are true.

Joseph Koberling was a brick mason who specialized in ornate and intricate fireplace designs. He built the restaurant for someone else, but took over the operations himself, doing everything from prep to cooking to cleanup. The Roaring Twenties were a big part of this structure, and photographs have surfaced showing flappers standing outside and signs that read "Music and Movies Free to Patrons." The Cave House was known as an alcohol-related establishment from Prohibition well into the 1960s. Bootleggers, moonshiners, and the like were often said to be the main reason for the place, and the "chicken restaurant" was just a ruse. The Cave House holds many secrets, like the column that was removed by a previous owner and was discovered to be full of silver coins. The mysteries that surround the house are many, and the stories it tells are hidden deep within the hills that it was built into. Other rumors about the Cave House claim the hidden tunnels were once used by the Ku Klux Klan to hide its victims. The tunnels are also alleged to be another mass burial site for victims of the 1921 Race Riot.

There was once a woman who owned the Cave House named Ella Walker, better known as the Rag Lady. She was often seen pushing a grocery cart through the streets of Tulsa dressed in heavy coats and layers of rags, even during the hot summer months. Legend says that she was not poor at all but quite rich, despite how she looked. She wore diamonds regularly but went crazy. The diamonds disappeared, and family lore claims that she hid them somewhere in the Cave House, and they have yet to be found. Ella was married to Bill Walker, a shade tree mechanic who would work on cars at the Cave. The couple did not have any children, but Ella was seen daily collecting trash, rags, and other items in her buggy. There was a legend that she ran a retail shop out of the Cave House, but just like the Rag Lady herself, much of the story is a mystery.

It is said that Ella still haunts the old house. A woman's sigh or whisper is often heard and has been recorded in the walls of the odd structure. The current owner, Linda Collier, once covered the upstairs windows with vinyl coverings during some construction. When her friends began to call her telling her that the look was very unappealing she went up to remove it and found the window to be covered in rags, which she did not put there. At first she thought her husband was trying to scare her, but when he swore against it, she did some research and found out that the Rag Lady would collect rags and scraps of fabric from the trash, wash them, and then hang them in the windows to dry. The discovery was startling.

There was yet another mysterious owner of the Cave House who was known as the Key Lady. While there are few facts known about her, she is one of the many enigmas connected to the house. The Key Lady reportedly traveled around town as a turnkey. People would hire her to check on their businesses and homes to be sure they were locked and secure. This was well before alarms and surveillance cameras were invented. She was very proud of her job and the sense of responsibility that came with it. Legend says she walked around with a huge ring full of keys proudly displaying them for all to see. It is believed she still roams the halls and rooms of the Cave House and if a visitor is not careful, she will take his keys. Guests have had keys in their pockets go missing. Loose keys would be found in the brush surrounding the home. There have also been reports of the faint noise of keys clanging in the house.

Another strange occurrence was the first night the current owner spent the night in the Cave House. She was awakened by the sound of wind chimes inside the house in the middle of the night. Since there was no wind to push the chimes, the noise that woke her scared her as she watched them sway and suddenly stop. It was the dead of winter, the windows were closed, and no fans were on. Clearly someone wanted her to know of their presence.

Owners and visitors claim to have been pushed by unseen forces and people have felt threatened. Previous tenants had a dog that would react to nothing and stare and bark at the walls. Another former tenant would frequently go a little nutty and jump off the roof into oncoming traffic. People who have owned or rented the home in the past are supposed to have gone crazy living there and become obsessed with the home. Apparitions of a businessman in a suit and tie have been reported, and a lady peering out of the upstairs window is also seen by passersby. Maybe one day all the mysteries of the Cave House will be known. Until that time, the public will continue to be mesmerized by the tales and possibilities of the house that has been on the Tulsa scene for decades. With the likes of the Rag Lady, the Key Lady, and perhaps Joseph Koberling still loitering, it is entirely possible that the once thriving speakeasy has even more unknowns yet to be discovered.

Tulsa Hex House

One of the best-kept secrets in Tulsa is that of the Tulsa Hex House. This is a creepy story that revolves around a woman named Carolann Smith and two ladies she held captive in religious slavery for eight long years. This is a story of mysticism, scandal, enslavement, lies, and deception. At 10 East 21st Street, there once stood a duplex that held some frightening secrets within its walls. Long known in Tulsa as the site of the former Hex House, the land where the house once stood is still causing a stir.

In the early 1940s, a story broke out that amazed and confused the people of Tulsa. Reports from neighbors about screams coming from a duplex on 21st Street along with "peculiar sounds and growling" emitting from the home were just the start of the puzzle. A maintenance man who was called to the house for repairs found a woman who was rooming in the basement where he was working. It was a very cold winter night and the girl was barefoot and ill clad. When he asked if he could extinguish the furnace pilot light to work on it, the woman told him it was her only source of heat. A neighbor of the Hex House said he had once seen an unidentified occupant cleaning a shotgun on the porch. Several others informed Tulsa police of an interment that occurred in which a casket was buried in the back yard. So what exactly was going on inside that house? The stories and rumors are rampant but, strangely, they are also true.

Carolann Smith was born in Indianapolis as Opal Mary Carey. Her mother died when she was nine years old, and her father raised her. They moved to Muskogee, Oklahoma, where Carolann met Fay H. Smith and married him in 1914. Her husband was a well-known oil field supply salesman, and they had two children between 1915 and 1919. Strangely, neither child lived past a few days of age. After the death of their second born, they moved to Tulsa in 1920. The next 20 years were witness to some bizarre events. In 1934, during the height of the Great Depression,

Fay Smith was laid off. Shortly after this devastating news in difficult times, he was found dead off Riverside Drive from what appeared to be a suicide. The blast that ripped through Smith's head was from a shotgun, and a twig was used to pull the trigger. His friends and co-workers were shocked at the news of his death and claimed Smith was not the type of person to take his own life. Carolann had a very large insurance policy on her husband and was given payment of the policy immediately following his death. Evidence came to light that Carolann talked to her husband at length about suicide just before his death.

At that time, the Smiths did not live at the duplex formally known as the Hex House. They originally lived at the Sophian Plaza, but it had changed management and the new manager did not like Carolann Smith. In an attempt to get Carolann to move, the new manager raised the rent. The trick worked, and Carolann moved to the duplex at 10 East 21st Street. Claiming the duplex was too big for her to live there on her own, she began making arrangements to have her father come to live with her. He lived in St. Louis, and she traveled back and forth regularly just before his relocation. Strangely, her father died before he made it to Tulsa. Carolann had a very large insurance policy on her father as well, and she was now living a very comfortable life from insurance payouts.

On a very cold day in February 1935, only a month after the death of Carolann's husband, a woman named Beulah Walker ran out of the duplex in a screaming frenzy right into oncoming traffic. She was hit by a car and died in a Tulsa hospital a week later. At the time of Walker's death, Carolann claimed that she was a nurse who lived with her. Carolann gave the funeral home no information on the woman other than that she was a widow and 45 years of age. Officials attempted to contact Beulah's family but were unsuccessful. Carolann Smith made all the burial arrangements. Smith was also the beneficiary of a large life insurance policed issued on Beulah Walker. After Carolann claimed Beulah as a "wealthy aunt," she extracted additional funds from the insurance policy and suspicions arose. An investigation by the insurance company revealed that Walker was an underpaid housekeeper for Smith. The additional claims were denied and the policy cancelled.

In 1937, Carolann Smith met a woman named Virginia Evans at a Christian Science bookstore. Evans was from a prominent family in Stroud, Oklahoma, where her father was a very wealthy merchant. The two women conversed regularly and soon appeared to be good friends. Virginia asked Carolann if she could move in with her.

A year later, in 1938, Carolann met a woman named Willetta Horner at a grocery store and an acquaintance was formed. Horner complained of an unhappy home life, saying she was alone and wanted someone to adopt her. She claimed to have had a very difficult and miserable childhood. Carolann convinced Willetta to discard her friends, associates, and family and move in with her. Willetta did just that. The woman worked in the area at local businesses, and everything seemed normal. Carolann successfully played it off as the three women being roommates, but it was later learned that this was far from the truth.

During the World War II, Carolann applied for and received seven ration books. She claimed some of the books were for her children and dependents, but her neighbors knew she did not have any children. One of the names given was actually that of her dog. The other books were in the name of her late housekeeper, Beulah Walker, and her deceased father and husband. Books were also issued in the name of Willetta Horner and Virginia Evans, the women who lived with her, and an 11-year-old nephew she claimed also lived with her. Fraud against the ration board was a serious offense, and an investigation was started. When Tulsa police conducted interviews, neighbors reported screams, growling, and other strange noises coming from the house. Police also learned of an apparent burial by the three women in the back of the house. This testimony resulted in a warrant. Indeed, they found a casket in the backyard that contained the remains of Carolann's dog, Bon Bon.

When police invaded the Hex House they found two women in the basement dressed very scantily and sleeping on egg crates, with very little clothing and no shoes, hungry, cold, beaten, and deprived. The women were Willetta Horner and Virginia Evans. The two ladies claimed they were "mesmerized" and "hypnotized" by Smith in what they referred to as a hypnotic swindle case. They claim a spell was cast against them to relinquish all their earnings to Smith so she could continue her lavish lifestyle. Rumors of cruelty and inhumane treatment surfaced, and it was noted that Smith conned many people out of a large sum of money. Insurance payouts from the dead that seemed to follow her and letters sent to Virginia's father claiming she was very ill and needed a nurse and the funds to support her well-being were her lifeline. She got tens of thousands of dollars out of the families she tortured. She had taken out insurance policies on the two girls just a month before police made their discovery.

Known today as the Mystery Case, the ladies' claims of a hex placed on them are how the duplex earned its nickname. After the story broke, former residents of the other half of the duplex came forward with stories of torture and craziness. A former tenant tells of a time when he was lured under a window on Smith's side of the duplex where Virginia Evans threw scalding hot water on him. It was also said that Willetta would pick fights with the residents and cause them much dismay and trouble. The women both admitted to have done these things, but at the direction of Smith, whom they never disobeyed. They claimed that Smith promised them life eternal in heaven if they did as she asked. They said religious indoctrination made them believe they would receive a great reward for serving Smith, who claimed that she was a healer and that she could save the women from a life of hell after they died. Smith plotted the girls against each other and they were enemies while living in the house, but each claimed that she did so at the request of Mrs. Smith.

Interestingly, Beulah Walker and Carolann's former husband, Fay H. Smith, were not the only people to die after some sort of affiliation with Carolann Smith. A total of seven people were found dead shortly after having some type of acquaintance with the Hex House mistress. Mrs. H.D. Folger, Carolann's sister, had recently died. John Evans, a former chief criminal investigator who investigated the death of Carolann's husband, died shortly thereafter. Captain Rains, who reportedly ran over Beulah Walker, died suddenly after the accident and, strangely, never spoke of the incident to family or friends. H.P. Browser, the Christian Science officiant who presided over the funeral home ceremonies, was found dead, and Mary Horner's corpse was discovered shortly after she came to Tulsa to look for her daughter, Willetta. Perhaps the moniker Black Widow would have suited Carolann Smith better, but Hex Mistress seemed to fit as well.

The story of Carolann Smith has more twists and turns than a carnival ride. During a raid of the home, when the women were found in the basement, police were also surprised to find enough make-up to fill up a drugstore and over 200 pairs of shoes. At a time when such items were rationed, Carolann felt she was entitled to have them. Willetta Horner and Virginia Evans worked during the day and turned over their paychecks to Carolann so she could maintain her lifestyle while the girls lived in filth. The women asserted that Smith contrived false sex stories to plot and alienate them against each other and against their own mothers. They claimed that Carolann manipulated them and instilled distrust in everyone they knew except her. The stories of Smith practicing her own strange hybrid religion and the sex scandals that included the girls she held captive were depraved. Police found sex toys and other items that made them speculate on the nature of the girls' relationship with Smith. Carolann would talk to them and drill them from morning to evening about things the girls claimed were "so terrible" they could not bear to repeat them. Again, the question is raised: what exactly happened inside the infamous Hex House? Carolann was never formally linked to all the deaths that surrounded her, but she was charged with obtaining money under false pretenses, subornation of perjury, mail fraud, and using false statements to obtain a ration book. When she was released, she left the state and has not been seen since. The tales of bondage, casting spells, and hexing that echoed throughout the trial has fueled intense interest in the Hex House since 1944.

The duplex was demolished in 1975, but the basement where the women were held captive is still there. It was filled with dirt and paved over, but some say the land is still hexed. The property became a parking lot for the Akdar Shriners, but the stories do not stop there. Tales of unusual activity still surround the old, empty lot including cars moving on their own and disappearing from where they parked. Others tell of parking their vehicle in the lot to return and find it running, windshield wipers on, and radio blaring without a key in the ignition. Cars seem to have a mind of their own when parked there. The lot now sits empty, abandoned, and lonely, but the enigma remains. There is a retaining wall that borders the property, and a fence has been erected to seal it from public use. Could it be all the strange things that happened on the lot are why it is permanently closed off? The retaining wall in front of the property still contains the original stairs that Beulah Walker used in her fateful walk into oncoming traffic. The wall also has the original stone materials that once matched the house. Are those stones holding the bizarre memories of what were once the most mysterious and sensational cases in the city of Tulsa? Something is.

The Brady Mansion

The large, Southern-style mansion located at 620 North Denver Avenue was the former home of one of Tulsa's most influential men, Tate Brady. Built in 1922 and sitting stately in the coveted and opulent Brady Heights historic district, the mansion is surrounded by rumors and stories of conspiracy, malice, racism, and malevolence. The home also had a reputation as the place to be among the elite socialites of Tulsa. Tate Brady named the mansion Arlington, after Gen. Robert E. Lee's home.

Tate Brady was known for many things. He was an entrepreneur, an oilman, and one of the incorporators and founding fathers of Tulsa. However, rumors abound that Brady was not the model citizen he was portrayed to be. He came to Tulsa in 1890 and opened a mercantile store offering to pay premium prices for hides, fur, and wild game. It was big business that earned Brady much wealth and prestige, enough that the entire neighborhood was named after him. Brady's wealth allowed him to own many vehicles, so he constructed a garage to house them all. This garage is located at 423 North Main Street and is now known as the legendary Cain's Ballroom.

Tate Brady's father was a soldier for the Confederacy during the Civil War. Brady was very proud of this and decorated his home to reflect it. He was a true Southerner, with murals throughout Arlington displaying the antebellum life. In fact, a large painting of Robert E. Lee was displayed on a mantel over the fireplace, where sons of the Old South would gather to talk, drink, and toast the general. Every year, on January 19, they would have a party to commemorate Lee's birthday. There was even a chapter of the United Daughters of the Confederacy that operated out of his home in the 1920s. During that time, it was not uncommon to see tables set up along the lawn to host lavish parties and bridge games in honor of Civil War figures like Robert E. Lee and Stonewall Jackson.

There was also a dark side to Brady's notoriety. Suspicions ran high that Brady was a grand wizard of the Ku Klux Klan. Given his social status and political views, the idea of Brady being a Klansman sadly would not have been uncommon for that era. The KKK was active and growing in Tulsa, and Tate Brady was said to be both an orchestrator and facilitator for the group. The church located across from the Brady mansion was said to have made a deal with the Brady family. Identical pillars front both the mansion and the church, and the story goes that the church was

This stately mansion, built in 1920, shows the opulence and wealth of oil baron and Tulsa entrepreneur Tate Brady. Coming to Tulsa in 1890, Brady opened a mercantile store and later a hotel. Being very active in the Sons and Daughters of the Confederacy, he often held tea and bridge parties on the front lawn of the mansion to celebrate the birthday of confederate general Robert E. Lee. After loosing his fortune during the Great Depression, Tate Brady committed suicide in the kitchen of the home and is said to still linger around the mansion.

given the leftover pillars in exchange for allowing a grand wizard to live across the street.

Several years later, the Brady family leased the mansion to the government and gave it up to house defense and service workers during the war in 1942. The dwelling was divided into a series of apartments, and Mrs. Brady saw the project through to the end to ensure every detail to perfection for those who would call the place home. However, the house quickly became dilapidated and over the years hosted some tragic deaths and unfortunate circumstances. Urban legend says Tate Brady's father died inside the home, and Tate Brady himself committed suicide with a self-inflicted shotgun blast to the head in the kitchen.

As the mansion continued to fall into severe neglect and disrepair, vagrants and drug dealers moved in and made it their home. Many deaths associated with drugs and drug-related crimes cursed the house and continued to increase the damage and bad reputation of the old home. The building was finally rescued in 1988, when it was purchased by Tim Lannom. During restoration of the old house, Lannom made some rather interesting discoveries inside. He noted some rather peculiar inclines in the basement. He traced them to their origins, knocked some holes in the walls, and found two hidden staircases with secret panels that had been undisturbed for over 50 years. Lannom restored the home to a single family dwelling once again and brought back much of the allure and grandeur that Arlington originally possessed. The house and neighborhood were placed on the National Register of Historic Places, Tulsa's first neighborhood to be so honored.

The colorful history of the Brady Mansion makes for a good story, but its walls also tell of times past when some of its residents never left. On any given spring or summer evening, someone walking past the Brady Mansion might hear the clanging of glasses, shuffling of cards, and idle chatter as if the lawn bridge games were still going on. Lights inside the home have been seen to turn off and on by themselves, when no one was in the structure. An upper veranda door has been witnessed swinging open on its own, with no one on the other side. Whispers and faint cries have been reported coming from the building in the middle of the night. Indeed, the mansion and its history will make anyone stop and question what the walls would tell if they could talk. Legends that continue to roam the halls, basement, and rooms of the old house tell of a time when the elite hid their secrets and used their power and prestige for their own benefit. The presence of those ghostly inhabitants who met a sudden, tragic, and untimely death still make themselves known today inside the Brady Mansion and remind us of their role in Tulsa's past.

Tulsa's Oldest House

Tucked away in Owen Park is Tulsa's oldest house. Its former owner, Sylvester Morris, was a farmer, carpenter, and Methodist minister for over 50 years. He was born in 1836 in Ohio and married Mary Mills in 1859. Together they had eight children. Morris was a Civil War veteran and was involved in General Sherman's famous March to the Sea, from Atlanta to Savannah, Georgia. He was often seen riding his horse and buggy wearing a large, floppy hat on his head. Morris ministered as far away as Tiger Hill in Broken Arrow and was an amazing philanthropist in his time.

When his first wife, Mary, passed away, he married Harriett W. Burton Smith Reagan at her residence in Indian Territory in 1894. She had five children, and together they had three more. Morris acquired a house and lot in Tulsa at 412 North Cheyenne Avenue in 1887 for $15 in a deed signed by the principal chief of the Creek Nation, Pleasant Porter. Morris had previously built a three-room home of native oak on this site, and it is believed to be the oldest house still in existence in Tulsa. It was moved to Pioneer Corner in Owen Park in 1976. The house was renovated but has been repeatedly vandalized with much damage done to the historic structure.

The truly sad and unusual part of this story involves the death of Sylvester Morris at age 79 in August 1907. He was building the house to help supplement his income and had a wagon full of lumber that he was transporting from the sawmill on Bird Creek near Skiatook. As he was taking the materials to his home in North Tulsa, two deputy marshals, C. H. Wilson and Frank McGlothin, rode up behind Morris demanding he stop the wagon. Morris was practically deaf and did not hear the demand. When they fired several shots over his head, he whipped his team and sped away, fearing vagabonds were trying to rob him. Five more shots were fired, with one of them hitting Morris and killing him. His horses continued on until they reached the Morris farm, where his wife found him dead and slumped over the wagon seat. Her cries and sobs rang out as she tried to make sense of what had happened to her husband. A coroner's jury found the two deputy marshals guilty of murder. During the trial, they claimed that they believed Morris was a bootlegger and therefore shot him when he refused to halt. They were later tried in the Muskogee court and acquitted of any wrongdoing.

Mary, Sylvester's second wife, died in 1921 at the age of 88 and is buried alongside her husband in Oaklawn Cemetery. The four-foot monument commemorating them is still in the graveyard with their names and dates inscribed upon it.

There are rumors that on some evenings you can hear Mary's cries from when she found her beloved lying dead in his wagon. Strange noises have been heard and lights have been seen in the house where there is no electricity. Now it sits empty and lonely on a little hill in Owen Park.

Rev. Sylvester Morris, Harriet Smith Morris, and her daughter Lyda stand on the porch of their home, Tulsa's oldest existing house. This photograph was taken around 1890.

TULSA'S HAUNTED MEMORIES

The Brady Heights Historic District

What was once "the place to live" in Tulsa is now again a thriving neighborhood. From territorial days until the 1920s, the Brady Heights neighborhood was full of young professionals and oilmen. The area received its name from W. Tate Brady, who was a pioneer, entrepreneur, and Tulsa developer. While he is held in high regard, it is also said that he had a dark side. Located just north of downtown Tulsa, Brady Heights was a chic place to live in early Tulsa. It extends along Denver and Cheyenne Avenues to Marshall Street, and most of the homes were built between 1910 and 1930. The wealth and prosperity of the homes is apparent with their bay windows, leaded glass, carriage houses, and large wraparound porches. Even the one house built prior to statehood shows the elegance of early Tulsa.

Brady Heights was the first residential neighborhood built outside the downtown area and was the exclusive domain of Tulsa's rich and well-to-do set. The neighborhood was the first in Tulsa to be placed on the National Register of Historic Places. It fell into severe disrepair during the 1960s and 1970s and was known as a place for vagrants, drug dealers, and drug-related crimes. The houses that once held Tulsa's elite were being destroyed by neglect and vice. However, the vicinity was brought back to life in the 1980s by caring citizens who did not want to see a huge part of Tulsa's history lost forever. In the 100-plus years this neighborhood has been in existence, it has seen its fair share of tragedy and misfortune. Such calamity is still apparent today in ghostly sightings that happen quite regularly.

On the 600 block of North Cheyenne Avenue was the home of Charles Reuter, who was murdered in 1912, shot to death by his wife and a former employee in a love triangle turned bad. Rumors stated that the wife wanted Reuter killed so she could continue her affair with the employee. Reuter is said to haunt the neighborhood, and witnesses have reported seeing him roaming the streets calling out for his unfaithful wife.

In the 700 block of North Denver Avenue is the ghostly residence of Jerome Cutchall, an oilman who died in 1930. While little is known about his death, his presence is said to linger through footsteps on the stairs and lights that seem to float in midair. It was said that Cutchall did not like children and did not have any of his own and because of this any family that moved into the house with children would quickly vacate as he made it quite uncomfortable for them.

In the 1100 block of North Denver there have been witnesses to children playing in a vacant house. One witness was awakened in the middle of the night by loud horseplay that was taking place in the yard. The eyewitness described the children as dressed in period clothing and called the police. Upon investigation, no children were found in the empty, abandoned house.

It seems that one of Tulsa's oldest neighborhoods still has residents of the past who do not want to leave a place they called home for many years.

The Greenwood District

Much like the Brady Heights area, the Greenwood district was also once a thriving neighborhood. It was called "Black Wall Street," home to wealthy African Americans. The area was known to be the most prosperous and successful black community in the United States. However, this once vibrant neighborhood was put to the torch in Tulsa's darkest days, the 1921 Race Riot. One of the bloodiest battles in the riot happened at a church known as Mt. Zion, located in the Greenwood district.

The Ku Klux Klan was very active in Tulsa in the early 1920s. In fact, John Q. Hyde, a national organizer, announced that the national headquarters would be located in Tulsa and attorney Earl P. Joyce was named head of the Tulsa chapter. On the evening of April 1, 1922, the Klan staged a parade in downtown Tulsa though denied permission by the mayor. Low-flying aircraft bearing a giant fiery cross were seen over the downtown area as Klan members marched in an orderly and silent fashion along the streets in front of thousands of spectators. Fearing the parade would fuel another riot, citizens of Tulsa sat silently and waited for the demonstration to be over, with a sigh of relief at the end. To everyone's surprise, it was a peaceful demonstration.

The Greenwood district had been burned to the ground during the riot and all that remains today are the eerie concrete foundations and stairs leading to them. Legends say that on certain cool evenings shadowy figures roam among the now vacant lots. Sounds of faint voices and crying can be heard on still nights. The area was eventually rebuilt but it never retained the notoriety it once had and those vacant lots and concrete foundations are a creepy reminder of what once was a flourishing, successful part of Tulsa's past, one that has not seemed to fully go away.

Three

THEATERS AND MUSIC VENUES

Tulsa Little Theatre

The Tulsa Little Theatre began when three forward-looking women wanted to create a social center for stage plays and musicals. In 1929, performances began in large circus tents. The structure was completed in 1932. Famous plays like *The Drunkard*, *Our Town*, and *All My Sons* were performed and produced at the Tulsa Little Theatre. In fact, Tulsa Little Theatre was the first community theater in America to produce *Our Town* and *All My Sons*.

The spooky little theater that sits quietly on Delaware Avenue just south of 15th Street lies among tree-lined streets in a thriving residential neighborhood. The houses that surround the theater are all brick, gingerbread-type homes that are historic in and of themselves. It is a quaint and trendy neighborhood, yet the theater has seen its share of tragedies, both real and surreal.

Renovations were done to the back stage and foyer areas in the late 1940s but were destroyed in a devastating fire that broke out just after the third performance of *The Women* in 1965. The very next year, the theater had another fire that forced productions to move to the Performing Arts Center in Tulsa as a permanent home. The actual stage and seating are located underground in what was supposed to be a basement, but due to the fires, construction was never completed, leaving the stage and seating still underground today.

Before the construction of an actual building, Tulsa Little Theater staged productions in a tent located on Delaware Avenue at 15th Street, as seen in this c. 1929 image.

The building went through several different incarnations in its life. It was at various times a Karmic church, the Delaware Playhouse, and Avondale Studios. Those changes brought many different owners, producers, performers, and visitors. Some of those past residents have imprinted themselves onto this location and can still be felt and heard today. Many musicians, actors, and stage personnel will tell you that the Tulsa Little Theatre is indeed haunted. From equipment malfunctions to lights mysteriously turning off and on by themselves to faint voices and images that make a person scratch their head, the Little Theatre is not just a landmark, but a very haunted one.

The ghost of a little girl named Sarah is said to roam the theater. Legend says that Sarah was performing in a recital here and afterwards ran out into the street in front of the theater and was hit by a car. Her injuries, unfortunately, proved to be fatal and she died. A former owner of the building claimed he would often get knocks on the door from residents of the neighborhood telling him his daughter was playing out in the street. The former owner was a single man who did not have any children. The current owners are still waiting for that infamous knock, but reports say that sometimes passersby can hear a little girl talking and singing outside the theater doors.

Another ghostly presence at the Little Theatre is that of a former director named George, who died suddenly and unexpectedly of a heart attack during a performance. George was said to be a prankster and many have been eyewitnesses to his jokes from beyond. A former actress told of a time when she went to retrieve props before a performance and found the prop closet empty. When she went to report the missing items, she found them all over the theater in inconspicuous places. During the night, when the theater was locked up and no one was there, the props were somehow removed from the closet and placed in various spots. Many believe it is George playing tricks on unsuspecting victims.

Other unusual activity at the theater includes files being misplaced, equipment malfunctions, lights going on and off on their own, and footsteps so loud they sent three men running for the door during an event. The sandbags for the curtains have been seen swaying on their own and have even fallen, crashing to the stage and barely missing a person. Voices and idle chatter have been heard from the backstage area, and ghostly apparitions have been caught on film during events. Children visiting the theater have claimed to see other children who were not physically there, and many have reported seeing the silhouette of George sitting in his chair. The stories and legends of the Tulsa Little Theatre add up to a big mystery.

The Brady Theater

Also known as the "Old Lady on Brady," the Brady Theater stands majestically on the corner of Brady and Main Streets in the thriving downtown district of Tulsa. It stands proudly in the city

The Brady Theater is pictured in one of its incarnations, as the Tulsa Municipal Theater. Located on the northwest corner of Brady Street and Boulder Avenue, the Municipal Theater was closed down when the downtown civic center was built. It later reopened as the Brady Theater.

Originally known as Municipal Theater, Tulsa's first convention hall was built in 1914 from a $100,000 bond issue passed by the citizens of Tulsa. The convention hall was later named Tulsa Municipal Theater and then Brady Theater. Mae West, Buddy Holly, Enrico Caruso, Chuck Berry, and many other famous people have graced the stage of the Old Lady on the Brady, which at one time was the largest theater west of the Mississippi River.

that grew up listening to the famous actors and entertainers who have graced its stage throughout the decades. Many of those performers have come and gone, but some really haven't left.

Built in 1914, the theater symbolizes the past wealth, vitality, energy, and problems of Tulsa. The intimate atmosphere and superb acoustics of the old structure make it one of Tulsa's best entertainment venues today. The cabaret style offers an alternative to formal concert seating, including an orchestra pit that is adjustable, allowing the area to be raised to floor level for additional seating or stage level for increased intimacy with the audience.

In 1910, Tulsa citizens were confident in the oil capital their city had become. Those barons of petroleum imagined a great city and a great entertainment facility to match. At 101 East Brady Street was the birth of Tulsa's first convention hall, boasting seating for 3,500 residents in the five-story high brick building surrounded by red brick streets. It was the largest theater of its kind west of the Mississippi River. Today, the Brady Theater retains its original classical architecture along with the nostalgia of days long past in pictures of famous entertainers that hang on the walls.

The Native American treaties of 1866 paved the way for the railroads crossing Indian Territory. In the 1880s, a railroad crossed the Arkansas River in a northeastern direction. Just a little over a square mile of downtown Tulsa, including tiny Brady Street, was paved in bricks parallel to the tracks. Like in most Southern towns at that time, the tracks divided the white and black sections of town. The Convention Hall was built just north and east of white Tulsey Town. As the settlement grew into a city by the mid-1900s, blacks accounted for 12 percent of the city's population. When Oklahomans wrote the state constitution in 1907, they included Jim Crow laws, which were about segregation and making things "separate but equal." About half of Tulsa's African Americans lived in the Greenwood district, which was also known as "Black Wall Street," and the other half lived with or on the property of their white employers. Racial tensions often ran high on the "white side of the tracks."

Veterans returned to the Greenwood district only to have less freedom and respect than they had received in France during the war. Black workers belonged to the International Workers of the World, an organization that had promoted communist equality since the 1870s. The local lodge was located at Brady and Boulder Streets on the corner opposite the Convention Hall. In 1918, white Tulsa policemen entered the lodge and arrested eight men for loitering, although all were organization members and were innocently playing cards and dominos. The only white person arrested was fined and let go; the seven blacks were held over for trial. Later that night, a mob of white men lynched the seven men.

African Americans attended performances and events held at Convention Hall but entered through "Blacks Only" entrances on the west and east sides of the building. Just inside were "Black" bathrooms and washing facilities. They even had their own seating sections in the balcony closest to their entrance. Ironically, those are some of the best seats in the house. Black performers and musicians could only use the small dressing rooms on the east side of the stage.

Wrestling matches, traveling minstrels, famous singers, orchestras, and actors all performed at the hall. In the first week of June 1921, William Jennings Bryan was scheduled to speak but his engagement was cancelled because one of the worst race riots in United States history had ripped Tulsa apart. The Convention Hall played a vital role in the race riots.

Legend says that some of the most prominent men of Tulsa and other deputized white men rounded up residents of the Greenwood district. They marched them through the downtown streets to the Convention Hall. White urban legend says that blacks were taken there and detained for their protection, while black urban legend says they were beaten and tortured inside. Surviving photographs support the black perspective and show countless victims being corralled into the theater's entrance at gunpoint with their hands in the air. Dr. Jackson, a black man, was killed on his way to the convention hall, and another man was murdered just outside the doors.

Several hundred men were escorted, or herded, into the building and the doors locked. What happened inside remains a mystery today; however, urban legend maintains that some of the 300 unaccounted for were thrown into the coal-burning furnace and others were buried in the walls and floors of the basement. In the late afternoon on June 1, 1921, the hall's population was gradually moved to other areas known today as the fairgrounds and old McNulty Park, an old baseball field. The Red Cross entered the building to nurse the injured victims, and a few stayed there up to a week. Nearly the entire Greenwood district was burned to the ground by fires set during the riots. The Convention Hall was spared because a white man owned it. Lynchings occurred in public view for all to see. Men were burned alive, beaten, hanged, and disgracefully mauled.

As African Americans began to rebuild homes and businesses, whites worked to forget about the death and destruction and sweep it under the proverbial rug. By the end of June, the Convention Hall was once again open for business. There is no doubt the Old Lady on Brady has witnessed horrific events. Its walls hold secrets to the infamous chaos that enveloped Tulsa, and the spirits that roam the theater are a testimony to the horror the structure had to witness. There is no doubt that the Brady Theater is one of the most haunted structures in Tulsa.

One of the famous men to grace the stage of the Brady was the Italian tenor Enrico Caruso. He performed at the theater on October 17, 1920. Being from Italy and never having seen an oil well up close, he asked the oilmen of Tulsa to show him one. Tate Brady and other proud oilmen took Caruso in a three-car entourage to a nearby city so he could see how the oil wells were developed. On the way back, all three cars broke down, forcing Caruso to walk back to the theater on what was a very cold and rainy day. Legend says that the Brady was sold out, and it was one of Caruso's best performances ever. He received a standing ovation and several requests for encores. Shortly after his performance at the theater, Caruso went back to Italy and died. Some say he was already sick with the lung disease pleurisy, while other accounts say it was that walk in the rain that led to the fatal disease. Lore says that Enrico's manager blamed Tulsa's weather as the reason for his demise and haunts the Brady Theater in retribution for his death.

There are many urban legends that surround the Old Lady on Brady. One recalls a stage manager who hanged himself in the rafters and is said to haunt the theater. His name, supposedly written on the wall in the attic rafters, only appeared after his death, to the surprise of owners and stagehands. The mysterious signature is said to have been put there by the manager on his ghostly quest for immortality and acknowledgment. Employees at the theater say they sometimes see a spectral shadow on the catwalk above the stage and believe it to be the distraught stage manager. Cleaning crews have witnessed and heard the slamming of doors in the restrooms as they clean. Faint voices and loud, startling noises permeate the old building.

The theater remained opened and was one of the premier concert venues in Tulsa up until the 1970s, when it closed due to the opening of the Convention Center. At this time, the theater was still called the Convention Hall. In 1974, Peter Mayo purchased the building and renamed it Brady Theater. Mayo made many renovations, including removing the segregated bathrooms "because they were creepy." The segregated entrances were also closed and he added a concession area to the front, creating a lobby. The front lobby has seen some of the most strange and unusual occurrences. Doors on popcorn machines have been seen to open on their own, glasses clang together, and items have fallen off shelving for no apparent reason.

Are the victims of the race riot the ones who haunt the Brady? Is the basement truly a makeshift grave for those who never left the building? Are discolored bricks evidence of the truth of this urban legend, or is it time that has slowly eaten away at the masonry, causing the discoloration? Is the stage manager the black shadowy figure often seen pacing the catwalk? Or is it the ghost of Caruso who makes his presence known to Tulsans for causing his untimely death? No one really knows, but the Brady definitely perpetuates the mystery of what happened within its walls.

The Cain's Ballroom

The legendary Cain's Ballroom is one of the most notable landmarks in Tulsa. Not only is it famous for the music it features but also the ghosts that roam the old building. Built in 1924 during the oil boom, the structure was used as a garage to house the many cars belonging to oilman Tate Brady. The garage was converted into the Lavure Ballroom in the late 1920s as a taxi hall for country music. In the 1930s, Madison "Daddy" Cains purchased the building and named it Cain's Dance Academy. It offered ballroom dancing lessons for only a dime. Nightly the doors would open, and droves of people would enter for a night of music, laughter, and ballroom dancing. In the evenings, recitals would be held so students could show off their newly honed dancing skills.

Built in 1921 originally to house the many vehicles of oil baron Tate Brady, this legendary structure in Tulsa has been an icon on the Tulsa landscape for decades. Cain's Ballroom is haunted by the ghost of Bob Wills and an unidentified female ballroom dancer. The employees and patrons alike will tell you that the music doesn't stop when the show is over.

Bob Wills and the Texas Playboys entertained at the legendary Cain's Ballroom. Their live radio broadcast through KVOO brought fame and notoriety to both Tulsa and Cain's. Fan letters from as far away as California caused KVOO to double its wattage, putting Tulsa at the country music forefront.

Daddy Cains would bring in bands from Texas quite frequently, but a favorite was the Light Crust Doughboys. In the 1930s, it was not uncommon for a band to be named after the product that sponsored them. The group's manager, Pappy O'Daniel, was said to be a slave driver and would work the band 50 or more hours in the factory and have them playing and practicing music late into the night. The weary lead singer got tired of the hard driving O'Daniel and quit the band. He moved to Tulsa permanently and was hired by W. O. Mayo, who would now become his manager. That lead singer was none other than the famous Bob Wills.

In February 1934, the first live broadcast of the new band Bob Wills and the Texas Playboys was sent out of the Cain's Ballroom. Every day at noon for nine consecutive years, this live broadcast would bring people from all over the country to see Bob Wills. His show was quite a popular act, and Wills quickly became known as the founder of Western swing. He would forever change and influence country music. The Cain's became known as "The House that Bob built." Before long everyone wanted to play at Cain's Ballroom, and after doubling the wattage at local radio station KVOO, Bob Wills became a national phenomenon. He was compared to the likes of Benny Goodman, Glen Miller, and Tommy Dorsey and was a huge success as a country artist. His radio show and his song "Take Me Back to Tulsa" hit the airways and put Tulsa and the Cain's Ballroom on the map. The live radio broadcasts ended in 1943, and Bob Wills headed to California to pursue his dreams of stardom. The Cain's wouldn't be the same for nearly 30 years. After his departure, the ballroom gained quite a reputation as a rough-and-tumble type of spot, nicknamed the "Crazy Place" and the "Rowdy Roadhouse." By the late 1950s, promoters avoided using the venue to host their music in fear of how disorderly the place had become. The *Tulsa World* newspaper reported that some of the toughest and bloodiest gang fights took place right outside Cain's front doors. A Tulsa city prosecutor declared the ballroom a menace and "more trouble than anything else in town" and wanted it destroyed. His wishes did not come true, and the Cain's continued to wreak havoc until the birth of rock and roll destroyed it. Throughout the 1960s, when Elvis was shaking his hips and rock and roll had made its appearance on the music scene, the ballroom struggled to stay open and eventually closed its doors. The building was purchased by W. O. Mayo and remained vacant for nearly a decade.

In 1972, an 83-year-old woman named Marie Myers purchased the building and tried to once again bring the grandeur of ballroom dancing back to the Cain's. Marie made the ticket office her bedroom, but her revival failed, so she leased the building out to different promoters who would put work into it. There were thus many squabbles over ownership.

Finally in 1976, a local concert promoter who always loved the old landmark purchased the building. Larry Shaffer bought the Cain's ballroom for $60,000, the proceeds from a Peter Frampton concert. He put another $40,000 worth of renovations into the structure and brought a who's who of popular music to Tulsa. Acts like the Greg Kihn Band, Huey Lewis and the News, Pat

Benatar, Talking Heads, and the Sex Pistols played at the Cain's and brought hundreds of people to the legendary taxi hall. In addition to rock concerts, Shaffer also hosted pig wrestling, mud wrestling, and other colorful events that added to the mystique of the building. It was at this time the employees of the Cain's noticed some weird things about the place. Disturbing occurrences such as dark shadows, glasses clanging together, and unexplained sudden equipment malfunctions were a nightly happening.

Throughout the 1980s, Larry Shaffer tried to sell the ballroom several times, even being offered as much as $400,000, but each time the sale would fall through. It is alleged that if Bob Wills did not like the potential owners, the sale just would not happen. Bob Wills was long gone by this point, but apparently he still oversees ownership of the house that he built. Again in 1982, when Shaffer brought his staff into the office to announce he was putting the ballroom on the market, a ceiling tile fell and with it came down very old fan letters to Bob Wills. Apparently Wills was making it known that he did not approve. Until Shaffer found an owner that Wills approved of, the sale would not go through. In 2002, prominent neurosurgeon Jim Rogers got the thumbs-up from Wills and purchased the building. He invested $1.2 million worth in renovations to bring back the original domed ceiling, and the Cain's was born again. It was placed on the National Register of Historic places and continues to be one of the leading music venues in Tulsa today.

The very first performance after renovations was a concert with Dwight Yoakam. That night, there were two ghostly sightings. During the renovations, the owners purchased an old textile building that was attached to the ballroom and put in a second bar and stage which they affectionately call Bob's Place. During the Dwight Yoakam concert, a young lady working behind the bar in the new addition was making a drink and went towards the end of the bar to throw something in the garbage can when she saw a lady dressed in a red ball gown standing and staring intently at her. The ghostly figure was transparent and startled the bartender, who quit right then and there. The former worker will not discuss the incident to this day, as it was too frightening. Later that evening, a gentleman wearing 1930s cowboy attire walked up to the main bar and asked the barback for some 10¢ popcorn. The barback laughed and turned to the lead bartender to ask about the popcorn and as they turned around, the man had vanished. The Cain's has not had 10¢ popcorn since the 1930s, and the man was not seen again the rest of the evening. The woman in a red ball gown is known as the Lady in Red, and while no one is absolutely sure of her identity, many claim it is the ghost of Marie Myers trying to bring back the splendor of the ballroom dancing scene she once knew. The old man walking around in old attire is said to be the ghost of Bob Wills. Legend says that he still makes his presence known to employees at the Cain's. He has been seen nodding in approval at workers cleaning the ballroom after a concert and his disembodied voice has been heard echoing through the building.

When the building is closed, workers claim to hear the faint sounds of ballroom music, voices like a party or crowd, and sounds of a woman calling out. When people would come out of the business offices wondering if someone had wandered in, no one could be found. Dark shadows have been seen passing through the bar area, and voices of a woman sobbing and crying uncontrollably have been heard in the ladies' restroom. Flickering lights that seem to have a mind of their own and equipment breaking down only to suddenly start working again are common at the legendary dance hall. With all the witnesses to such bizarre events, there is no doubt that the Cain's remains home to more spirits than just those being served up.

Four

COFFEE SHOPS
AND BARS

The Old Hotel Fox

Once known as the booming Hotel Fox, this building is quite a little secret in Tulsa. Built in 1906 and having a very elusive history, it was one of the only structures left standing after the 1921 Race Riots due to its ownership by a white man. Known as a first-class hotel along Main Street in downtown Tulsa, it was a warm, inviting, and comfortable place. Many visitors from around the world who came to Tulsa for the International Petroleum Exposition spent the night at Hotel Fox. The successful lodging would eventually become a popular brothel and later a dirty flophouse lending shelter to transients and drug abusers for only $5.

In what used to be the lobby of the old hotel now sits a trendy restaurant named the Brady Tavern which has seen its share of ghostly encounters. The decor, which includes dramatic draperies, hand painted murals, and bright colors, adds to the allure. Directly above the restaurant is a part of the building that has never been remodeled. Walking through the halls of the empty and abandoned second floor is like stepping back in time. Rickety swinging doors open on small, enclosed rooms with just a single window that have not changed in over 80 years. A person can almost hear the sounds of glasses clinking, cards being shuffled, and the whispers of propositions to the young cowboys who frequented the brothel.

J. M. Hall built Tulsa's first general store, which also acted as a post office, and was Tulsa's first postmaster. He helped lay the foundation for Main Street and contributed to the city of Tulsa in many ways. The store was also used to hold city meetings after a devastating fire destroyed many of the buildings downtown.

The madam of the flophouse was a middle-aged woman named Ms. Moore, who was gaining a reputation as being shady, mean-spirited, and untrustworthy. The operations she ran out of the rented space would eventually be the cause of her demise. She was quickly becoming known for the sinister atmosphere she created from the late-night parties, prostitution, and substance abuse she allowed. The landlord eventually shut down her operations, and rumors claim she was very upset at the forced eviction. Not knowing when or how she died, current tenants of the building say Moore has stayed behind to prove her dissatisfaction. Others claim she is worried about what people must have thought of her and fears judgment. Therefore, she lurks in the dark corners and shadows of the building making her presence known.

There are also rumors that murders, drug overdoses, and deaths caused from overindulgence are the cause of the unusual activity in the building. The staff has reported such oddities as single-stacked glasses thrown to pieces on the floor with no visible cause and no one around them. They have witnessed two apparitions in the building as well: a man in a long trench coat and bowler hat standing in the doorway between the cafe and restaurant, and a tiny older woman dressed in black, who has been reported by employees and bartenders in the same area.

Employees have said that they often hear their name called by a disembodied voice and that stereos and televisions come on and switch channels even when unplugged. In fact, it got so intense one night, a bartender was closing up and felt the walls closing in on him as he heard voices. The unsettled barkeep quickly exited the building and did not return until daylight. Another employee reported a time when she was working by herself and went to get something in another room only to return and find the water running in the sinks and the doors standing wide open.

Strange noises, disembodied voices, and aggressive energy seem to be prevalent in the old building. One of the evening bartenders told the current owners that after he closed up and locked the doors he realized he forgot his cell phone. When he returned to the building, disarmed the alarm, and grabbed his phone, he heard two men having a very loud conversation. This encounter led to yet another employee leaving the building in a rather hasty manner.

However, some of the most bizarre experiences at the old hotel occurred to a former dishwasher and a chef at the restaurant. The dishwasher said he was clocking out after the lunch rush one afternoon when he was stopped dead in his tracks. As he approached the main dining room, the temperature dropped to a very cold chill, making it almost unbearable. He reported a loud buzzing noise and what he described as a charged, electrical field so powerful he was unable to touch the register to clock out in fear of being shocked. The strange atmosphere soon vanished and went back to normal; however, after that experience the dishwasher didn't last long at the café.

A former chef at the restaurant, Rick Miller, took up residency in the vacant second story of the building to be close to his kitchen. But Miller would have strange nightly experiences that made his tenancy at Hotel Fox very short. He told of hearing the sound of cowboy boots coming up the stairs and roaming through the halls and foyer as he tried to sleep. One night the footsteps came into his room and stopped at his bed. While the sounds themselves were quite frightening, the final straw came when he felt someone sitting at the end of his bed. He watched the corner of his mattress form an indentation, with no one there. This encounter sent the chef fleeing the building after living there for less than four weeks.

It seems that if someone visits the old Fox Hotel, they may get more than they pay for. Patrons and employees alike have been spooked by a past that appears to have never left. The building's history is vague and mysterious, and it could be that the spirits who still roam there are trying to reveal its secrets.

The Gypsy Coffee House

The Gypsy Coffee House is in a mysterious building at 303 North Cincinnati Avenue in downtown Tulsa. The three-story brick building was once the corporate headquarters for Gypsy Oil Company. After sitting abandoned for 25 years, it was purchased by Bradley Garcia, who renovated it into a hip coffee house and salon. The venue hosts poetry readings and local music. The building has some interesting energy to it, but its ghosts are mischievous and rude.

The Gypsy has had a long history of strange dealings. The oil company was at the center of much controversy and scandals dating back to 1917. It was brought to court many times for tax fraud, illegal drilling, and evasion of workman's compensation claims, all of which dogged the company throughout the 1920s. The biggest of the scandals occurred in 1919. A wrongful death suit was brought against the company concerning Clarence Edgar Ginn, who had been crushed to death by a drilling machine. His widow continued the suit over a course of 12 years, but the case was ultimately dismissed.

In the years since the coffee house has occupied the building, many strange things have been reported. Employees claim to see ghosts of both children and adults. The apparitions are common at the old establishment. It is said that they really like to harass the current owners and workers, especially new employees.

One of the ghosts most frequently seen at the Gypsy is that of a former janitor, Tony, rumored to have died under veiled circumstances on the property. Many claim that he had been set up and others insist he was killed intentionally, but all agree that Tony lingers in the halls of the coffee house. Employees have recalled seeing the apparition of a young, good-looking blond man in a long black trench coat who dissipates into thin air as he approaches one of the building's exits. Other specters include a rather nasty-tempered nine-year-old girl whose name is unknown. People often see her dressed in present-day attire and most frequently in an area of the coffee shop known as the cloud room. She has been known to scream at the employees, demanding a cookie.

When things don't go her way, she gets very upset. One of the workers saw her skipping around a coffee table, and two patrons also witnessed the carefree apparition. Those customers never returned to the Gypsy. The cloud room is said to be her favorite place to sit and play, and some employees refuse to break in that area. Employees have also witnessed three little boys laughing, running, and peeking over the counters at them. There is a storage area in the men's restroom where some claim to hear boys laughing and carrying on all the time. Employees have come out of the kitchen to find coffee cups all over the floor near the counter, while never having heard a sound and being alone. Many people claim to have the feeling of being watched while at the coffee house.

It is said that when the oil company occupied the structure, it offered a childcare facility for workers. When a fire destroyed the daycare, not all of the children escaped. Could it be that the kids who were not lucky enough to escape the flames are still looking for a way out of the building? Could they be wandering and playing, still waiting for their parents to get off work and take them home? Whatever the case, the Gypsy seems to have a presence of spectral beings who can't or don't want to leave.

Empire Bar

Built in the 1920s, the Empire Bar sits at the corner of 15th Street and Peoria Avenue. The building is rumored to have once been a firehouse and ambulance shelter because of the large garage doors on the front that are opened to provide sidewalk cocktails during nice summer evenings. No documents confirm its use as a firehouse or ambulance shelter, but the stories certainly make for some interesting conversations about yet another Tulsa gem that has an elusive and obscure history. In the late 1800s, this was Creek Reservation land. During the allotment of land to Native Americans, a young woman believed to have been named Sentinel was given this share to develop. Later Cyrus Avery bought the property and sectioned off the neighborhoods that sit behind the Empire Bar today.

The Empire Bar is located in the Cherry Street District, not far from other purported haunted locations. The area is known to have a lot of ghostly activity. Before the development of legitimate businesses, saloons, brothels, and poker houses lined the dirt street, and some believe the name Cherry Street derived from such activity. During that time, the vicinity was rich with wild and illegal activity that seems to have left its mark on the businesses located there today.

Reports of strange activity at the Empire Bar come from both patrons and employees. Two customers once reported that as they approached the bar, the bartender leaned over to get ice from a bin and a soccer trophy above him came crashing down to the floor, narrowly missing his head. The patrons described the incident as if the trophy had slid forward, lifted, and dropped from the

Though scratches mar this photograph, Tulsa's skyline in the 1960s features signs of the oil boom.

top of the bar like someone grabbed it; yet it was too high up, and no one could physically reach it. The trophy, although a bit banged up, is still in the bar today, glued together and standing as a broken reminder that some guests are not welcome at the Empire. The two witnesses left rather abruptly, without their drinks.

Another odd incident was noticed by a waitress when a patron had matches thrown at him. The man moved a few times to avoid the nuisance, but the fiery threats followed him and he eventually left the bar. Unable to believe what she had seen, the waitress asked the owners to review the security cameras, which showed flickers of fire descending from the ceiling of the building onto the unsuspecting patron, tormenting him until he left. Upon inspection, the matches were found to be long wooden ones like those used to light fireplaces, which the bar had at one time; similar matches were found on the rafters in the ceiling.

Strange activity like wineglasses being thrown off the bar have cost the owner some money. People have claimed to be touched and have their necks blown on, and inexplicable cold spots have been said to occur. The owner said that she once received a 5:00 a.m. phone call from the bar when no one was there. The company that monitors the security system confirmed that the alarm had not been disarmed and the building was still locked. Yet the owner's caller identification showed that the call had come from the bar. The scoop from the ice bin has been found leaning against the walk-in freezer, carefully balanced on its handle, even after being used. Typically the scoop is left in the ice bin, but it is often found in the same odd place and in a position in which it could not possibly have landed had it fallen.

Disembodied sounds of a man whistling have been heard in the building when patrons had yet to arrive or had long since gone home. During renovations, while working on the upstairs part of the building, workers heard what sounded like a man's voice and the sound of marbles or ball bearings rolling across the roof. The direction in which they heard the balls moving was opposite to the slant of the roof.

One day the owner was showing a new employee around the bar. While they were in the back room, they could hear chairs moving around in the main bar area. Annoyed with the sound, the owner yelled out for whoever it was to stop. When the noise kept on, the two went to see who was making the racket and saw all the chairs in front of the locked front door, with a linen service company employee patiently waiting outside. The owner began to move the chairs out of the way, and the new girl began to cry.

It seems that there is a woman attached to the old Empire Bar, and some say it could be Sentinel. According to locals who frequent the bar, it is not uncommon to have a ghostly experience after you go home as well. Staff have claimed a female ghost goes home with new employees for a while just to check things out and see if they are fit to be an employee of the Empire. One employee claimed he kept thinking he forgot something and would repeatedly unset the alarm and go inside to check on things. After the third or fourth time, he heard a deep woman's voice mocking and laughing at him. The laughter followed him home that evening.

While there is no significant history attached to the building to justify such a haunted reputation, the Empire is not for the faint of heart. Those who don't mind having a billiard ball thrown at them or a man tugging on their clothing may have what it takes to be an employee at the Empire.

Rehab Lounge

The corner of 18th Street and Boston Avenue is a chic area of bars and restaurants on the outskirts of downtown Tulsa. Mostly occupied by popular clubs and nightspots, the structures that crowd the area have been around since the early 1900s and have witnessed hundreds of businesses come and go.

One particular building, located at 39 East 18th Street, has had many owners and different tenants, but all of them have one thing in common—ghost stories. Once a skate shop, among other things, the building has mostly been home to local nightclubs. The frequency with which it changes tenants has been attributed to the annoying resident spirit. Former business owners, even those many years apart in their occupancy, all maintain that a ghostly figure is lurking on the east side of the building. Rehab Lounge, the current occupant, has the same disturbing stories that are decades old.

The odd-shaped building has two stairwells, on the east and west sides, that lead to upper terrace and loft areas. Two separate terraces on the east and west sides of the building look down on the bar, common area, and dance floor below. Just underneath the corners of the terraces are the women's and men's restrooms. Some people claim that a man once jumped off one of the terraces with the intention of landing on the bar. Apparently he missed the bar and hit his head, breaking his neck and causing his untimely death. Since that time, everyone who has rented the building has claimed there is a presence inside that will never go away. Within just the last decade it seems this building's spectral presence has become more active. The frequency of odd things happening has greatly increased, causing some to get a bad feeling and others to refuse to work there.

What used to be the DJ booth on the east terrace has now become a storage closet due to the number of sightings and ghostly activities that have taken place there. One busy evening before the DJ moved her booth to the opposite side, she abandoned her station and refused to return. When asked by the owner of the club why she was not working, she claimed that she could not work in the booth. Further probing caused the DJ to tell the owner that while she was up there she could feel someone tapping her to the beat of the music. Feeling uncomfortable but not scared, she reached the final straw when something unseen slapped a CD case out of her hand and onto the floor. This incident sent her sprinting downstairs to grab a drink and get away from whatever

This photograph of downtown Tulsa was taken from a rooftop in the 1960s.

it was that was tormenting her. Despite the trouble to move all the equipment, the DJ did so just to get out of the east terrace. The booth was moved to the west side, and she was much more comfortable and said she was not bothered again after that.

The owner of Rehab Lounge continued to hear stories from his staff that something was going on. One bartender told him that when she was working alone after the happy hour crowd had left and before the evening crowd arrived and there was no one else in the building, she could see a shadow in the loft area and felt as though she was being watched. She said it got so intense that she could feel something directly behind her, breathing down her neck. It was quite a relief when a patron entered the bar, as the ghost was more likely to cause trouble when someone was there by himself.

One time the owner went to the bar about 3:00 a.m. after closing to pick up the nightly deposits and paperwork. When he arrived, he found the bartender there with several people. When he asked why there were people at the bar after hours, the bartender claimed he could not close down alone because the place was too scary. His friends were there to wait with him and keep him company until the owner arrived to take over and lock up. The employees of Rehab Lounge were claiming that things were getting too weird in the building so the owner, who had not felt anything unusual, decided to take over a shift and see for himself what the staff was getting so upset about. He was ready to meet the culprit face to face one Tuesday evening.

It was just after the happy hour crowd and before the night crowd arrived when the owner found himself alone in the building. He hadn't felt anything out of the ordinary and so turned on the television. When he did so, the sound was so low he couldn't hear it, so he turned up the volume. The sound of the show could still not be heard, but a ringing in his ears began. As he continued to turn up the volume, the ringing got louder. He said afterward that it didn't hurt, he just felt uncomfortable being unable to hear the television. Finally, with the TV at full volume and the ringing in his ears even louder, he could hear only a muffled mumbling and could not understand why there was no sound at a setting that would normally be far too loud. He had been playing with the remote for what seemed like five or ten minutes when one of the bartenders walked in the door. Just as the door opened, the ringing stopped and the television was blaring so loudly the owner could not hear the bartender ask him why the volume was so high. He turned it down and explained what happened, and as he looked at the clock he realized that it had not been five or ten minutes but rather an hour since he first turned on the television.

The ghostly presence in the building did not often reveal itself to employees or owners, but when it did, many claim the experience was too intense to want to repeat. A few sightings of a dark figure standing against the wall by the men's room have been reported.

One evening as the owner was closing up and his girlfriend was waiting with him, she suggested they stay for a few more drinks. The owner said he was feeling nervous and did not want to stay and "upset the ghost." Thinking he was talking nonsense, the girlfriend agreed to leave anyway. They closed up the bar, and he set the alarm and said a loud goodbye to the room, almost mocking himself as he talked to the presence he could feel was there. He made a comment that he was leaving and the place would be closed up the next day so the ghost had the place to himself. With a nervous laugh, the owner locked the door and turned to walk away when the jukebox inside the bar came on at full volume. He and his girlfriend could both hear it. The song that came on was a live version, and they heard the very loud applause of a crowd. Feeling a little freaked out, they left and did not go back inside that night.

Another time when the owner was closing up, he realized he had forgotten to turn off some lights. When he went back inside, a dark shadowy figure was leaning up against the wall next to the men's room. The owner claimed it acknowledged him by tilting its head toward him. The shock he felt sent him fleeing the building without turning off the lights or setting the alarm. Driving very quickly to a nearby convenience store to gather his thoughts and nerves, he ran into an old friend. Feeling rather flustered, he told the friend of his strange experience. Since he did look like he had just seen a ghost, the friend offered to go back with him while he turned off the lights and set the alarm. The two men went back to the bar to shut it down and everything was normal. The owner was shaken by the experience and finally knew his staff was not exaggerating about what they had gone through.

Could the dark shadows and other disturbances be the spirit of the man who accidentally killed himself? Whatever it is, it certainly caused a stir.

Five

HOTELS AND LODGING

Camelot Hotel

The Camelot Hotel, also known as the Camelot Parkside Inn or Camelot Inn, was built in 1965 by Ainslee Paurait. Completed in two years, the eight-story, 330-room hotel was a large pink castle with a King Arthur theme. The hotel even included massive iron gates, a moat and drawbridge, and a swimming pool in the shape of the tip of a medieval spear. The lobby of the hotel displayed armor and other medieval furnishings that would send visitors back in time. They could almost picture jousting tournaments, epic battles, royal feasts, and knightly romance as they strolled through the hallways. During the construction of the hotel, a large sign was placed atop that read "Total Electric." The sign was removed after two electrical fires threatened the building even before it opened. Legend says the Camelot was cursed or doomed from the beginning, yet others disagree due to its success.

In 1968, the Kinark Corporation purchased the property for $68 million, the largest real estate purchase in Tulsa at that time. The hotel played host to many weddings, receptions, proms, reunions, and club meetings. It seemed everyone wanted to be at the Camelot. Many famous people spent the night in the popular hotel, a favorite of locals and visitors alike. In 1971, President Nixon stayed there when he visited Tulsa, as did President Ford, Elvis Presley, and Lt. Gov. George Nigh. It was featured in the 1982 movie *Tex* with Matt Dillon, based on the novel by S. E. Hinton,

One of the finest lodgings in Tulsa, the elaborate and sophisticated Camelot Hotel (or Camelot Inn) was famous for its "Total Electric" sign. Elvis, President Eisenhower, and many other famous people stayed at the Camelot.

a native Tulsan. Tulsa's elite could be seen at the ever-popular Sunday brunch buffet that was served at the hotel. It was not uncommon to have 200 to 300 people visit after church. Those unable to attend could watch it through a live weekly television show. Indeed, the Camelot was the embodiment of luxury and class.

By the early 1990s, the glory days had come to an end for the famous hotel. People were disappointed in the rundown, dilapidating building. It was sold several times to different owners who continued to operate it as a hotel. Foreclosures and a string of negligent owners soon allowed the Camelot to deteriorate into a place where prostitution rings, drugs, and scandals were the norm. Once a place of distinction and grandeur, the Camelot became dark, mysterious, and sinister. The hotel was rapidly developing a bad reputation when Dep. Sheriff Wesley Cole was shot and killed in the parking lot in the line of duty. What should have been a routine check turned into a shoot out with a criminal who was breaking into cars. The curse of the Camelot was being realized. Bad news seemed to surround the building. After the structure was struck by lightning, it was closed for good in 1992. The big pink castle remained empty for a few years and became a hang out for drug addicts and vagrants. In 1995 it was purchased by the Maharishi group, which claimed it intended to turn it into a "Peace Palace," a place to practice transcendental meditation, and a teaching institution. However, the building remained empty and continued to fall further into disrepair for several years. What had been an icon on the Tulsa landscape was now a sad reminder of times gone by.

Looking lonely and deserted, the Camelot lost its appeal but gained a mysterious reputation with claims that it was run by a cult and also haunted. Claims of sudden sickness when near the site, lights turning on and off with no power to the building, and apparitions peering out of top-floor windows became more and more frequent. Toward the end of the Camelot's life, rumors abounded that strange happenings were taking place. Feelings of being watched or followed were felt by some of the building's last visitors. Whispers of suicides, drug overdoses, and other deaths circulated about the hotel. The vibe and energy had turned sour and cold. There was even an urban legend that a pack of hellhounds lived inside the hotel and protected it. No one dared to go inside in fear they would be attacked by the wild dogs.

The Camelot was demolished by the city of Tulsa in 2008 and the vacant lot is almost as spooky as the old building that once stood there. Tulsans mourned the loss of a local icon, but, as with anything, all good things must come to an end. The question is, do they really leave?

TULSA'S HAUNTED MEMORIES

The Mayo Hotel

The prestigious Mayo Hotel was built in 1925 by brothers John and Cass Mayo. They had a vision of an elegant meeting place for Tulsa's elite and left no detail undone. Their vision to build a first-class hotel that exceeded the expectations of even the pickiest of patrons eventually came to fruition. The Mayo was one of the only places to get a drink during Prohibition and the first to have ceiling fans, polished limestone, and running ice water in every room. Indeed, the Mayo was significant in the growth and history of Tulsa.

Built as a replica of New York City's opulent Plaza Hotel, the Sullivanesque, Chicago School structure has been a part of Tulsa's beautiful skyline for over 85 years. The 18-floor building was the tallest in Tulsa from 1925 to 1927. It boasted 600 luxury rooms, and some very famous people have wandered its halls. Visitors such as John F. Kennedy, Bob Hope, Babe Ruth, Elvis Presley, Charlie Chaplin, and Mae West have spent the night there. President Nixon also gave a speech there once. It was a popular venue for galas, weddings, proms, receptions, and gatherings of all types. The Mayo was the place to be seen, and the affluent of Tulsa made it their home and party place for over five decades.

Businesswoman and Tulsa socialite Trula Austin was a resident of the Mayo for nearly 25 years. She was one of the few local women who owned a business when she inherited Mrs. DeHaven's flower shop after the owner was in a fatal car accident. Patrons and employees alike loved Trula Austin. Said to be a very vivacious lady, she was known as Tulsa's best hostess and was noted for the Christmas parties she threw every year. Frequently seen in her red sequined dress and feathered hat, she was know as the Woman of the Mayo or the Mayo Socialite. Austin assisted the hotel in gaining a reputation as a vibrant meeting place and one of the biggest and best party venues in town.

Eventually the Mayo's lights began to dim as war, recession, and economic hardship faced the citizens of Tulsa. Soon the Mayo closed its doors and remained abandoned and destined for demolition. During the 1980s, a few renovations were attempted, but the building was left unoccupied and bare for more than 30 years. The former glory and grandeur that was the Mayo was now only a silent memory on the corner of 15th Street and Cheyenne Avenue in downtown Tulsa.

In 2001, the Snyder family of Tulsa purchased the distressed building and has since brought it back to life. With over $40 million dollars in renovations, the Mayo's lights shine bright again. The restoration project has brought the Mayo back from the dead to be one of the premiere venues in Tulsa for a weekend getaway or large event. The terrazzo and marble floors were returned to their original luster, and the grand staircase and other beloved features were restored to the hotel's original splendor. The 8,000-square-foot Crystal Ballroom, located on the 16th floor, was also

Built by brothers John and Cass Mayo in 1925, the Mayo Hotel was ahead of its time in detail, luxury, and extravagance. The two brothers set the bar in quality with the construction of a hotel that reflected their promise and commitment to the city of Tulsa. Many famous people including Elvis Presley and President Nixon stayed at the Mayo, and it quickly became "the place to be" for weddings, reunions, and special events.

refurbished. In fact, intricate plaster molding was sent to a company out of town to be returned to its original 1925 appearance.

The Mayo is now back to being the gem the city remembers. Future generations will get to enjoy this timeless piece of architecture that previous Tulsans were privileged to experience. So much of the old hotel is present in the newly renovated venue. The exposed air ducts are made from salvaged metal from the hotel's original water tank and boiler system. The hotel has 102 luxurious guest rooms, 76 loft apartments, seven meeting rooms, and a restaurant affectionately named Trula, after the Mayo's own socialite Trula Austin. The top floor of the hotel contains a penthouse that leads to a rooftop garden and a view of the city that is breathtaking. The 1920s elevator doors have been restored and feature the original Mayo logo. The past is alive and well at the Mayo—in more ways than one.

There are many legends and rumors that surround the grand hotel. Apparently, the past has never left the Mayo, and the spirits of times gone by still linger in the halls and rooms. Stories endure of a jealous wife whose confrontation of her husband and his mistress in the hotel resulted in gunfire that took the lives of those involved in a crime of passion. Tales of a woman walking around the parking garage, only to disappear into thin air, have long been told. Could it be the mistress who was shot dead, or possibly the Mayo's first lady, Trula, who continue to visit the site? During renovations, Mexican construction workers were said to run from the building yelling "Fantasma! Fantasma!" and refuse to return. Disembodied voices, faint apparitions, and strange occurrences are alleged to be present at the Mayo.

So those who book a romantic weekend getaway or plan an event at the Mayo Hotel should take note that they may be watched over by past tenants.

Mincks-Adams Hotel

The beautiful Mincks-Adams Hotel is located in the heart of Tulsa's historic business district. Built in 1927 during the International Petroleum Exposition, the Gothic, Italian Renaissance, and Baroque-decorated structure was built by I. S. Mincks and displays the wealth and opulence of early Tulsa. Its architectural style was the infatuation of many early Tulsa builders who often used decorative motifs in their visions of luxury and affluence.

The Adams Hotel, as it became known after a 1935 liquidation sale, was lost to the owner during the Great Depression. It has 13 floors, a full basement, and a penthouse. The glazed terra-cotta veneer seen on the interior stairwell, coffee shop, and lobby reflects a time when these materials boasted of extravagance.

While the history of the building itself seems benign, there was some tragedy and mystery in its past. In 1931, Orlando Halliburton either jumped, fell, or was pushed from the top floor to his death on Cheyenne Avenue in what many believe to be a murder. A rich oilman, Halliburton was said to have lost everything during the Great Depression when the stock market crashed and the city was gripped with poverty and despair. Whether his fall was an accident or not, it seems that Halliburton still roams the building and makes his presence known to many who work and play there. The cafe is reported to be the scene of strange things—from glasses falling off a shelf by themselves to strange dark figures seen lurking around corners.

The building is now occupied by many businesses, from law offices to cafes. Reports of ghostly apparitions, equipment malfunctions, and radios that turn off and on with no apparent cause are common in the old building. Visitors have supposedly witnessed water turning on by itself in the restrooms and had the feeling of being watched while inside the property. Night workers have claimed they could hear the elevator running, although a code is required to get the elevator to work and investigation found no one inside the car. Heavy footsteps on the stairwell were reported along with doors slamming and faint voices when no one was in the structure. Each time the building was checked, it would appear to be empty. It seems that Orlando Halliburton or possibly I. S. Mincks is keeping an eye on the building and its inhabitants, both past and present.

Inn at Woodward Park / Bed and Breakfast

Located across the street from beautiful Woodward Park in Tulsa is a charming bed and breakfast at 1521 East 21st Street. Currently known as the Inn at Woodward Park, the hostelry saw its former glory during the Roaring Twenties and oil-boom success. Much like the other homes in the Brookside and Swan Lake area, the inn takes guests back in time to when Tulsa was the Oil Capital of the World. However, this luck, wealth, and prestige eventually came to an end, and the Great Depression took its toll on Tulsans.

It was a time of desperation, hardship, and economic downfall so bad that many lost their homes, unable to pay for them. The inn's history and the history of its prior owners is so elusive and obscure that if its walls could talk, they might tell some shocking stories. The structure sat empty and lonely for many years, and there are tales of only two former owners, both of whom died inside the home. The few known facts only increase the mystery and intrigue. One story of a previous owner says they had no heirs and the house sat empty and lonely for many years. The other tells of a couple who died inside the house and deeded it to their daughter. Legend says the daughter wanted nothing to do with the house and simply let it go, again leaving the house empty and alone, perched upon a small hill and staring into the city that left it behind.

Today, the Woodward Park area is a popular and trendy neighborhood with shopping, dining, and nature all within steps from each other. The house sat dilapidated and destined for destruction until it was rescued in 2003. The listing for the home stated it as a tear down or total renovation, with damages and repairs that far exceeded normal expectations. Mark and Janet Mobbs purchased the dwelling and spent nearly three years and thousands of dollars renovating it. Once repairs were completed, the new owners added a 1920s decor to the interior, and the home was alive again. The bed and breakfast officially opened in December 2006, and guests could once again enjoy the grandeur of the home's past. Walking into this historic home is like stepping back in time. The basement door that is located in the entry takes visitors down a flight of steps and into an area that appears to have once been servants' quarters. The chain lock on this door is often seen moving on its own: perhaps a former servant is passing through? Also at the entry is the original wood staircase that takes guests to three bedrooms, private bathrooms, a sunroom, and sitting area. The windows of the upper floor offer a scenic view of Woodward Park across the street. The three bedrooms upstairs are referred to as the Hollywood, Jazz, and Moroccan Rooms. It seems that, in true Hollywood fashion, that room gets most of the attention.

During the renovations, the owners experienced some strange phenomena. A plumbing contractor working there one afternoon was seen quickly gathering his tools and abruptly leaving the home, claiming his leg had been tugged and pulled by an unseen force. He never returned to finish the job. Other strange things such as doors opening and closing on their own and the faint sound of an old phone ringing have been reported. The current owners did not disclose the odd events they witnessed during renovations, in an attempt to not scare potential guests. However, it did not take long before guests told the owners about some strange and bizarre things they experienced themselves, all of which occurred in the Hollywood Room. Such things as a remote falling off a dresser or nightstand by itself, to items like glasses and other personal property being moved from their spots were reported. Ironically, two separate guests experienced similar things in the Hollywood Room. Claims of strange dreams seem to frequent the guests in this room. One guest said it was the best sleep she ever had and had dreams of a man taking her flying. This only came to light when the guest asked if the home had any ghosts. When the owners told the guest they had experienced some strange things at times, the guest said a man told her the house was a place of healing, and she believed the house to be haunted.

A mother and daughter who came to the Inn at Woodward Park made reservations for three days. After the first night when they came downstairs for breakfast, the owner found them packed, purses in hand, and ready to leave. When he inquired if there was anything wrong, they said they could not stay there because the noise kept them awake. They described the noises as sounding like something being thrown around the room. Another time, a mother and daughter who stayed in the Hollywood Room had breakfast the next morning and then went shopping. During breakfast their conversation was normal and polite and nothing was said about anything strange occurring overnight. When the pair returned from their shopping trip, the daughter remained in the car while the mother retrieved her belongings. The guest explained to the owners that the daughter refused to stay there another night and got a room elsewhere for the rest of their stay in Tulsa. The mother, however, did not leave and stayed in the room with no complaints or problems. She said her daughter refused to talk about the reason for her hasty departure, but she herself thoroughly enjoyed her stay. One guest at breakfast one morning asked the owners who Harry was. The current owners, having been able to find very little history on the home, did not recognize this name. The guest then told them she had been awakened in the middle of the night by a man who was very angry and throwing things around the Hollywood Room. When the guest asked the man what he was doing there and what his name was, the man replied his name was Harry and that this was his house. The guest said she felt a little disturbed but not scared even though the man was quite visibly angry and upset.

In 1906, St. John's Hospital was built on a lot next to the house. In 1921, Ma Barker's gang killed a night watchman at the hospital during a safe robbery. The watchman's son was involved with the robbery that led to his father's death. While he did not shoot his father and had no intention of anyone getting hurt, he was a party to the crime. The son was named Harry. It is believed that he is the angry man who has been witnessed throwing things around the Hollywood Room, possibly in despair and guilt over the death of his father. If Harry once lived in the home, it could explain the strange experiences owners and guests alike have had.

Those looking for an exciting and mysterious lodging experience in Tulsa might check out the Inn at Woodward Park. They should ask for the Hollywood Room and tell Harry not to disturb them as they sleep.

Six

TULSA'S HAUNTED SCHOOLS

Bellview School / Lincoln Plaza

On the corner of Peoria Avenue and Cherry Street is where the first stoplight was erected in Tulsa. At the southeast corner of this intersection is a three-story brick building that is now a thriving commercial structure. At one time, this building was Bellview School, Tulsa's longest-operating school (from 1909 until 1990) and the first major structure built on Cherry Street. The original building was outside of the Tulsa city limits and had no running water or restrooms. In 1914, the school was renamed Lincoln, a name the building still bears on the south entrance. The elementary school was closed down in 1990, but its famous graduates include Tony Randall and William Boyd, famous for his role as Hopalong Cassidy. The school once had a bell tower, but it was removed in 1967 after being struck by lightning. After the school closed in 1990, it remained empty for three years and reopened after it was renovated into retail space and renamed Lincoln Plaza.

The old school was renovated and divided up for commercial use and now has everything from a popular bar to salons and restaurants throughout the plaza. As soon as the renovations were done and businesses began to occupy the building, strange things started to occur. The sound of children laughing was often heard and the rustling of papers (as if being shuffled) emitted from

Belleview School,
Tulsa, Okla.

Seen here on November 25, 1915, Bellview, Tulsa's longest operating school, was located at Fifteenth Street and Peoria Avenue. Originally designed and built to open, the windows were permanently sealed shut after an accident in which a little boy fell out of a third-story window and died. That boy still haunts and roams the building.

the walls of the structure. There was an instance where a glass flew off a shelf in the bar of one of the businesses located in the building. One day, a patron of one business was sitting patiently in the waiting area when he saw something very disturbing. He noticed a small child, dressed in black slacks and a coat and with short hair, crawl through the window. That was not the disturbing part. When he asked the receptionist if there was a patio out on the roof, the receptionist told him that there was no patio. He was adamant about what he saw, but as he argued he was surprised to find out that the windows do not even open! Apparently, a small boy fell to his death from this window in the building in the mid 1900s and legend says that the windows were permanently sealed shut afterwards to keep a tragedy like that from ever happening again.

One of the businesses in Lincoln Plaza is a deli that has had its own share of strange occurrences. One of the managers recalls seeing the same ghostly image that was seen by the patron at the other business. The two witnesses have never met or spoken to each other but have both seen the ghostlike little boy wandering around the grounds of Lincoln Plaza. Two strangers citing the same apparition in one location is quite compelling. The manager of the deli claimed that she was stopped dead in her tracks while taking out the garbage. To her surprise, she found a see-through apparition of a little boy dressed in black slacks and coat with short hair standing in front of the dumpsters. She was so shaken that she dropped the trash and ran back into the building. When another employee came out to put the trash in the dumpster, he did not see anything. The workers at the deli have also told about strange happenings and occurrences in the building. A television in one of the rooms would mysteriously turn on and off by itself at random times. The day manager would continually get frustrated with the night manager due to lights being left on. The night manager would adamantly deny leaving lights on, even going so far as to check them several times before leaving just to make sure they were indeed off. However, even with the multiple checks, the day manager would find them on when opening up in the morning. The faucet in the women's bathroom is also said to turn on full blast on its own when no one is in the bathroom.

Evening janitors have reported sightings of a "small dark figure" roaming the building. It seems the Bellview schoolchildren have left some energy behind. It also appears the little boy who lost his life at Bellview still roams the halls and grounds.

University of Tulsa

Originally named the Presbyterian School for Indian Girls, the college was started in 1882 in Muskogee, Oklahoma. It was a small Indian boarding school that was chartered in 1894 as the Henry Kendall College and Presbyterian Women's Board of Home Missions. Due to financial problems, the school moved to what is now its current location in 1907, the same year Oklahoma

Named after the primary benefactors, Robert and Ida McFarlin, the historic McFarlin Library, pictured here around 1930, has been the most notable structure on the Tulsa University campus. Haunted by a ghost that is affectionately referred to as "Farley," the old structure underwent several renovations and is said to be especially creepy at night. Books that fly off the shelves, hands that touch you on the shoulder, and other unusual happenings have been recorded at this decades-old building.

became a state. In 1920, it merged with McFarlin College to become the University of Tulsa. The university is internationally known for the bachelor's, master's, and doctoral degrees it awards in programs such as petroleum engineering, law, and natural sciences. However, that is not the only thing the school is known for. Tulsa University has long been reputed to be haunted by former students and alumni who lurk in the halls, dorms, and facilities.

One legend that follows the school is that of former president Dr. J. Paschal Twyman, who was said to have hanged himself in his seventh floor office. Another tale about a student who failed all of his classes and jumped off the building to his death makes both students and faculty a little nervous.

Kendall Hall is supposed to be haunted by a past resident advisor whose ghost still wanders around her former dorm. The girl had just completed a team-building ropes course and went back to her room. She committed suicide after overdosing on medications and left her phone off the hook. Residents of the dorm allege they will wake up in the middle of the night to the noise of a phone taken off its hook and are chilled when they find their own phone has been placed off the hook as well.

However, one of the most famous ghosts at the University of Tulsa is the one affectionately known as Farley, who wanders the McFarlin Library. It seems no one knows who Farley is, and many speculate it could be the ghost of McFarlin himself. Perhaps the ghost is a former student who is doomed to the library he should have been studying in when he was alive. Whoever it is makes his presence very well known. Books that jump off the shelf or are found rearranged cause problems for the librarians. Workers and students alike have reported papers and files misplaced or missing completely. Every time, the strange occurrences are blamed on the mischievous spirit of Farley. One evening, while a librarian was working late, she heard whistling. Thinking the cleaning crew had arrived, she went to greet them only to find herself alone. When she returned to her station and started to work again, the whistling resumed. Another story is that of a cleaning lady who came running out of the media services room after seeing an apparition of a man wearing a graduation gown. That cleaning lady never returned, but that did not stop the sightings of this strange man who wandered the library.

Another haunted area is Tyrell Music Hall. It is said the hall has its very own pianist, who will give performances after closing—when the lights are out and everyone is gone. One unsuspecting visitor to the hall heard the sound of beautiful music playing, and when he turned on the lights, the piano keys sounded as if they were slammed in a startled and angry manner, but no one was there.

The Honors House is said to have some misfortune attached to it. Tradition says that a group of depressed, drunk students jumped to their deaths from the roof of the house. Current students claim there is a hostile feel to the house, and some even called it demonic due to random paranormal activity that has been witnessed. Objects being thrown across the room, lights flickering, and doors that slam and lock on their own are the legends of this dormitory.

The questions of whose phantom images these are will forever continue to be a part of the mystery, one that gives the school character and makes people wonder who is there and why. Some say McFarlin was not happy with the additions made to the original building and so causes trouble and confusion in response. Whatever the case, Farley is held at least partially responsible for strange and bizarre things that go on at the University of Tulsa. While it does not seem that the school has a tragic past, it does seem to have a haunting presence. In fact, the university has had abundant paranormal activity.

Will Rogers High School

Built in 1938, the beautiful architecture of the Will Rogers High School reflects art deco flavor and pizzazz. Located on East Fifth Place, the school was built by the Tulsa Public Schools system and designed by Joseph R. Koberling Jr. and Leon Senter. It was named after the humorist Will Rogers. Placed on the National Register of Historic Places, the building not only holds a history of academics but also one of intrigue and mystery as well.

In the auditorium, a man has been seen wearing a white penguin tuxedo. He is often said to be wandering around both backstage and on stage areas and is rumored to be the specter of a former band director who died of a heart attack during a performance. Ironically, he was performing Bach's "Come, Sweet Death," and it was his first and only performance on that stage.

Dr. Carl Barnett died on April 23, 1974, and many students claim to see his ghost lurking around. Janitors or students staying late for detention or other activities have seen Dr. Barnett's ghost. Could he be longing for a repeat performance or simply hanging around to watch the performances at the school today? No one really knows. However, reports of him and a small person in white continue to permeate the school and will forever be a part of its past and future.

Old East Central High School

Founded in 1904, East Central High School was part of an independent school district prior to statehood. It was incorporated into the Tulsa Public Schools shortly thereafter, and after being vacant for a while, was eventually converted into a business. Since that conversion, strange things have been said to happen. From lights flickering on and off to files being moved and water faucets left on in the public restrooms, unexplained activity has taken place and earned the building the title of being haunted.

Some say it is the ghost of Doris Dixon who moves trashcans into the hallways at night or creates the sounds of footsteps in the corridors. She is blamed for making the elevators go up and down by themselves and for the faint sounds of music that seem to emanate from the walls. It was in the early 1930s that Doris lost her life in the basement swimming pool. There were mysterious circumstances surrounding her death, and many believe she remains in the building because of her untimely demise.

Workers in the building sometimes refuse to go in at night, as the building is known to be extremely creepy. Some even claim that looking at the engraved stones on the building and calling out to Doris will conjure a faint outline of her face on the brick of the year she was supposed to graduate. Could Doris still be hanging around the old building? With all the eyewitness accounts of strange phenomena that take place at East Central, it is quite possible.

Seven

LOCAL TULSA CEMETERIES

Oaklawn Cemetery

The large corner of land at 11th Street and Peoria Avenue in Tulsa is widely known as Tulsa's first cemetery, named Oaklawn. This was not, however, the original graveyard. Tulsa Cemetery was Tulsa's first cemetery, designated at Second Street and Frisco Avenue in 1882. When a road was needed in the area, many headstones were moved to the property at 11th and Peoria. All of those headstones date from before 1902 and marked the burial sites of Tulsa's pioneers. Grave markers were moved, but the bodies were never excavated, leaving human remains behind that are still being found today. In December 1905, Oaklawn was chartered and named the city's official cemetery.

Oaklawn was originally farmland owned by Alvin Hodge, a principal chief district inspector and Tulsa's first tax collector. The Creek allotment treaty allowed Hodge to give the land from his family farm to the township of Tulsa in 1902, prior to statehood. There was a condition in this allocation that if it were not used as a cemetery, the land would revert back to the Creek people. Oma M. Hodge was interred in the family's farmland in 1900, making hers the first burial here. She was only two years old.

There are many noted pioneering Tulsans buried at Oaklawn, including Rev. Sylvester Morris and his wife, Mary, owners of Tulsa's oldest house. Col. Edward Calkins, the first mayor of Tulsa,

An interesting assemblage of people lines up for a photograph in the H. R. Johnson Family Cemetery.

lies at Oaklawn, as do S. G. Kennedy, Tulsa's first prominent doctor, and a Mr. Orcutt, who developed Tulsa's first amusement park, complete with roller coaster, which is now Swan Lake. Tate Brady also rests here. There is also the grave of four-year-old Celia Clinton, who died of the scarlet fever that was raging through Indian Territory in 1904. Her parents were so bereaved that they established the Celia Clinton Elementary School in West Tulsa in her honor.

The southwest area along 11th Street towards the bridge is Potter's Field, a location used to bury the indigent and unidentified for many years. Legend has been passed down that many Race Riot victims are buried there as well. Written evidence, including funeral home records, confirms that African American race riot victims are indeed buried in unmarked graves in Oaklawn. Only two headstones identify actual victims; many of the others were laid to rest by strangers, so there were no markers placed or graveside services performed. No family members were present at the burials, as most of them were still being held under armed guard at various detention centers. Many of the victims' families never found out where their loves ones' final resting places were located.

Tulsan Clyde Eddy was 10 years old at this time and was an actual witness to the mass burials. He has been interviewed many times about his experience and is a reputable source of information on the subject. Eddy recalls waiting for the workers to take a break so he and a friend could peek into the large wooden crates. What they saw disturbed them as the crates contained several bodies of race riot victims piled inside.

Is Oaklawn cemetery haunted? Many believe that it is, as claims of disembodied voices, apparitions, and spooky happenings are reported at the graveyard. The landmark will always be a reminder of a horrific event that took place in Tulsa still being made worse by mass unmarked graves being found around the city: once again, a testimony to the unsettled pioneers of Tulsa's past.

Sparky's Graveyard

On 91st Street in Tulsa between Yale and Harvard Avenues, tucked away in a little corner, is an old cemetery known as Sparky's Graveyard. Located across the street from Jenks School, it carries a legend of a haunting by a former caretaker named Sparky. Some claim he was an albino who was rumored to be psychotic and is known to still scare people off the property with his unusual demeanor. Reports say Sparky has glowing red eyes that follow a visitor around, making them so uncomfortable they abruptly leave. Other tales claim Sparky to be a headless Native American who rides around the cemetery on a horse, chasing off unsuspecting visitors. Other witnesses claim to see a man standing or kneeling among the trees and wearing a large hat. Observers also say shadowy figures lurk around the spooky grounds, and claims of having hands slapped by unseen force have been reported, as have wet footprints that mysteriously appear on the concrete. It appears something is going on at Sparky's graveyard, but what it is remains to be seen.

Timberidge Cemetery

On a hill about six miles east of Catoosa on highway 412 is Timberidge Cemetery, also known as Haunted Hollow. Local lore says a little Native American boy had stopped to tie his shoe on the side of the road while riding his bicycle and was hit by a car and died. The boy was buried in Timberidge Cemetery and is said to haunt the area. Shortly after the boy's burial, motorists would report a boy riding his bike in the road at the top of the hill. Some would swerve to miss him and others claimed that as they approached the hill, they could feel their car hit something and hear a loud bang. When the driver got out to see what happened, they would find bloody handprints on their car but no explanation for them. Police reports are frequent in this area and have revealed damage to vehicles caused by an unknown source. The Catoosa Police Department also gets frequent phone calls about a careless boy on a bike in the area. Among the multiple accounts of strange occurrences on Timberidge hill, there are reports of nosebleeds while traveling through the area and feelings of illness such as sour stomachs, loss of feeling in legs and torsos, and temporary paralysis.

Whatever the reason, Drivers through this area should be sure to watch for a little boy on his bike and try not to hit him.

Eight

OTHER STRANGE PLACES IN TULSA

The Center of the Universe

There is a pedestrian bridge in downtown Tulsa that some claim is the exact center of the universe. Once the old Boston Bridge, it connects Archer with First Street (the same Bloody First Street discussed in chapter one). The bridge was built in 1930 for automotive use, so drivers could go over the train tracks. The Center of the Universe itself is a large circle in the center of the bridge, directly above the tracks, that measures 30 feet in diameter and is decorated with 13 rows of bricks.

There is an interesting acoustic effect at this location. When someone stands in the center of the brick circle and talks aloud, the sound creates an echo. While that may not seem unusual, anyone outside the circle will not hear the echo, only a normal voice. Some assert that the circle illustrates a secret form of alternative energy. Scientists say the spot demonstrates parabolic reflectivity.

Another thing that makes this area unique is the large statue named *Artificial Cloud*, located just south of the Center of the Universe circle. Created by Native American artist Robert Haozous, it was the 1991 Mayfest design and represents the rise of the industrial age in Tulsa. Many people find the statue alluring or mystifying for different reasons. The bottom of the statue has shackles that are a representation of early days, when Indians were often shackled and tortured. Legend says that the restraints have magical properties if banged against the statue at midnight on Halloween. On the south side of the statue are a section of humans without hands and airplanes going in many different directions. This design is especially unsettling because of what it faces: the Bank of Oklahoma Tower, which is a scale replica of one of the World Trade Center towers destroyed on September 11, 2001. The building was designed by noted architect Minoru Yamasaki, who also designed the World Trade Center. Many people find the 1991 statue eerily prophetic of the terrorist attacks in 2001.

Just northwest of the Center of the Universe is the old Union Train Depot. Today the old building has been renovated and is the home of the Oklahoma Jazz Hall of Fame, but the structure dates back to 1929 and was designed by R. C. Stephens. It is rumored to be haunted. The depot closed down and started deteriorating in 1967 but was saved in 1983 when it was restored and made into office space. Those who had offices in the building claim it was haunted with some rather unusual activity. Disembodied voices, moved objects, and strange sounds and smells have been reported.

The Moon

On a long stretch of road off 111th East Avenue in Tulsa, between Memorial Drive and Sheridan Road, is a wooded area known as The Moon. How its nickname derived, no one knows, but the legend of The Moon states that in those woods is where the Murdock Mansion once stood. Decades ago, the mansion burned down, leaving only a swimming pool, tennis court, fireplace, and part of a staircase as witness to the elaborate home that once stood there. Vandals, vagrants, drug users, and other troubled persons made it their home for many years as it sat neglected. This site has been reported to have some very strange activity associated with it. Reportedly, Devil worship was conducted here. Many people report that the minute they step onto the property, they are overcome by an eerie or queasy feeling in the pit of their stomach that makes them sick and gives them tunnel vision. Others claim they get so frightened that they become confused and end up lost in the woods, and a young lady supposedly once fainted from fright. Today the tract is used as commercial property, and people still claim to get spooked when visiting stores located on the spot where the mansion once stood. Some even contend that before the shell was torn down to make way for commercial structures, the fireplace would light up and quickly go out, causing trespassers to get so scared they would have trouble finding their vehicles, and that while looking they were being chased or followed by something unseen, causing them to get lost for a short time.

Early Tulsans pose outside one of the city's first grocery and general stores around 1890.

Southwest Boulevard / Red Fork

Southwest Boulevard on the west side of Tulsa around 41st Street is also known as Red Fork. In the late 1800s, many people flocked to Tulsa hoping to get a piece of property in the land allotment by the federal government. Two of those people were Dr. J. C. W. Bland and Dr. Fred S. Clinton in 1895. Both men moved to the area with the purpose of creating a hometown medical practice. Bland convinced his reluctant wife to drill for oil on her land, and the Tulsa oil boom was set to begin. Experts were predicting that the ground under Tulsa was rich with oil, but few believed it. The good doctors wanted to see for themselves. It was June 25, 1901, when the men struck Tulsa's first gusher and within 48 hours more than 2,500 hopefuls flocked to Red Fork with dreams of becoming rich.

With the good, however, came the bad. Ruthless groups collectively known as "oil men" had made their way to west Tulsa. Investors, spectators, gamblers, lease hounds, and many others could not be accommodated because of the lack of hotels and were sent into town. At the time, the Red Fork and Southwest Boulevard locality was not a part of Tulsa; it was separated from the city by the Arkansas River. With the influx of population to the area and no modern facilities, those who chose not to go into Tulsa made living space wherever they could. Conditions were said to be deplorable, and the district was concerned about disease and death. Eventually brothels, gambling houses, and saloons were popping up, and the outlaw way of life ruled the times. With so much activity in the late 1800s and early 1900s, there is no question as to why Southwest Boulevard and the Red Fork area is said to be haunted.

Located on the corner of Southwest Boulevard and Xenophon Street is the shell of a building that used to be an old gas station. Drivers passing this lonely piece of property can still see remnants of the murals that once decorated the exterior walls. The premises have been abandoned for decades. Back in the winter of 1969, when it was a working gas station, a brutal murder took place within its now gutted walls. A 16-year-old named Bobby was working there when a man came in and committed an armed robbery. Bobby was said to have been acquainted with the robber and promised not to identify him to the police. The thief told the boy he couldn't trust him or take the chance of getting caught. He forced the teen into a back storeroom, where he shot him to death. The criminal was caught and found guilty. He was sentenced to death, but it was later reduced to life in prison. Since the property was abandoned, it has become a hangout for vagrants and curious kids. Sightings of Bobby's ghost manifesting at the site have been widely reported. Perhaps the teenager is unhappy with the sentence that his murderer was given. Regardless of the reason, it seems the boy still wanders about the old store.

The Hall General Store was started by J. M. Hall in the 1880s. Hall, also known as the "Father of Tulsa," came to the city in 1882. His intentions were to work on the railroad with his brother, but he noticed how quickly Tulsa was growing and opened the first general store—located in the Redford district. His generous contributions to the city of Tulsa also included starting Tulsa's first church and public school systems.

Several residents in the Red Fork area report that their homes are haunted as well. Some claim that apparitions of cowboys or women in long dresses have been seen along with strange noises, smells, and inexplicable activity. It does seem as if the area of Red Fork and Southwest Boulevard has some secrets that have yet to be revealed.

Riverside Drive

A main corridor running north and south in Tulsa is known as Riverside. It is a recreational area located along the Arkansas River close to downtown, where people rollerblade, run, and walk along the trails. The space features a community park, Frisbee golf tournaments, and many other activities. It is quite a popular area and one that some claim to be haunted.

On the north side of the river is a route known as Whiskey Road, which used to lead straight to Fort Gibson. Bootleggers, peddlers, and other groups would get their whiskey from Fort Gibson and travel down this highway or run the whiskey on boats down the Arkansas River. Federal agents would frequently work the trail in an attempt to bust bootleggers, thieves, and smugglers. Their coverage of Whiskey Road was highly successful, and agents caught and jailed many who were illegally carrying liquor and drugs. Those who did not fight were given severe sentences for their crimes, yet others would not go down so easily. Much blood was shed on Whiskey Road, and it is believed those past criminals still haut the area of Riverside Drive.

At the intersection of 31st Street and Riverside Drive is the site of the first known trading post in Tulsa, established in 1848 by Lewis Perryman. That post was the only thing left standing after Tulsa was overrun during the Civil War.

In the 1960s, Tulsa voters were urged to pass the "River Lakes Park Plan," an idea to beautify the area along Riverside Drive. The project failed miserably due to flooding issues and the mess created. It was not until 1974 that the area got the facelift citizens had been wanting when a sales tax vote promised money to make massive improvements to the park.

There are several urban legends concerning the Riverside area. Tales persist that several bodies of race riot victims were dumped into the river to hide them from the official count by the Red Cross. Although there is no concrete evidence of this, the story has haunted the area for over nine decades. One elderly Tulsan remembers riding in his grandfather's truck when they were both approached at their windows and had guns held to their heads. They were told by unidentified men to load bodies into the truck and dump them into the Arkansas River. The men who forced his grandfather to do such a horrific deed threatened both their lives if they did not comply. The man remembers the fear in his grandfather's eyes and the shame and disappointment he felt as he reluctantly dumped the bodies.

Riverside was the site where Fay H. Smith committed suicide with a self-inflicted gunshot wound to the head. Smith was the husband of the mistress of the Hex House, Carolann Smith. Some claim he still wanders the area and makes people feel as if they are being watched and followed. Could an eerie presence in the park be Smith or could it be victims of the race riot who were dumped like old waste into the river? No one knows, but many agree the energy around the site is "heavy" at times.

However, the haunting of Riverside does not only belong solely to those race riot victims or those who took their lives in desperation. Many believe buried gold and treasure lies along Riverside that old prospectors would literally kill to find. Folklore tells of old Spanish pack train riches that are supposed to be buried along the riverbank. On New Year's Day in 1933, the *Tulsa Tribune* did a story about Spanish gold along Riverside Drive. It said that just south of the cottonwood tree between 11th and 13th Streets was the location of a buried cache. In 1904, dowsing rods were used to try to find the treasure. The rods did find a natural spring and along with it two very old shovels. Many people were purportedly run off and terrorized by treasure hunters protecting what they believed to be their prize.

Another Tulsa resident tells of a time when he was a child growing up along Riverside Drive. He and his friends would explore the drainage system underground. One day they came across a door with a chalk mural of the goddess Isis and a shrine of candles and talismans to honor her. They checked the door, which opened, and followed a hallway to find themselves in a boardroom. A guard found them and, as it happened, the boys were in the basement of a local bank. They often wondered what the door was doing there, as it seemed to be an escape route of some kind, another mystery along Riverside. The boys went back to the door the next day to find the shrine gone, the chalk drawing of Isis erased, and the door welded shut. They also claim the underground tunnels were the site of satanic rituals where animal sacrifices would take place and said it was common to find remnants of such rituals as well as punk and goth bands playing music there as well. Does all of this mean Riverside is haunted? It may not, but it adds creepy elements to an area that has mystified Tulsans for years.

Owen Park

Many people say that the Tulsa parks system literally began with a bang due to a massive explosion that occurred on January 23, 1904. A young man in his twenties was seen in his horse and buggy loading and unloading nitroglycerine around 4:00 p.m. that day. He had one of the most dangerous jobs of that time as a shooter, or well borer. It was a lonely but well compensated position.

In the early oil boom, a shooter was someone who would load nitroglycerine into a bored well spot, where it was presumed that oil could be found. The shooter would tamp it down and shoot it into the well to see if black gold would rise from the earth. On that chilly day in January in 1904, Virgil McDonald was doing this job when the aforementioned explosion ended his life. It was estimated that nearly 875 quarts of nitroglycerine exploded, blowing away McDonald and leaving pieces of his flesh around the vicinity, but only enough to barely fill a shoebox. The explosion was so powerful it was heard and felt over 15 miles away and even as far as Claremore, Oklahoma, about 30 miles away. It blew out the glass in the windows of the nearby business district and caused damage to homes in the nearby neighborhood. Due to his occupation, McDonald did not have a wife or significant other. Many women stayed clear of shooters for fear of becoming early widows. Having no family and being somewhat of a loner, he did not have an obituary, funeral service, or memorial. Virgil McDonald was left in pieces at what was to become Owen Park.

The land at Owen Park was originally owned by a man named Chauncey Owen, whose name it bears. Owen was allotted 160 acres of land after his wife Martha, a Creek woman, passed away. Owen and her beneficiaries were assigned the land and surrounding neighborhood where Owen Park is located. Prior to statehood, the land was used for public events, but it also was used to store nitroglycerine. On August 18, 1909, the city of Tulsa purchased the land from Chauncey Owen and officially declared it as a park. The ravine that remained from the devastating explosion was made into a lake, known as Owen Pond, that many now frequent.

The stories and legends of Owen Park are numerous and varied. There are reports of a dark figure walking around the lake that many believe is the restless soul of Virgil McDonald. But that does not explain the sightings of a ghostly little boy. On a regular basis, witnesses claim to see a little boy presumed to be around age six. He is described as wearing pre-1940s attire and running and screaming up and down Easton Street in the quiet hours of the night between 2:00 and 4:00 in the morning. Many speculate on why the boy is so distressed. Some believe he witnessed the explosion, and others say his grief and despair come from the house fire he survived, but no one really knows. Easton Street ends at Owen Park.

In 1910, the city of Tulsa sold five acres of land at Owen Park to the Tulsa Vitrified Brick Company. Chauncey Owen tried to fight the sale and even took the case as far as the state supreme court. He was afraid that the land sale would be detrimental to the health and well-being of Tulsans and worried that the hole the company would dig would be filled with water and lead to physical harm and become a breeding place for mosquitoes and disease. The Oklahoma Supreme Court found in favor of the brick company, and shortly thereafter Owen's fears came to fruition. A young boy drowned in the brick pit, long after it was deserted. The pit was filled in and later covered by the highway that runs east to Sand Springs.

Three reports of ghostly occurrences have been shadowing Owen Park since the early days of statehood. Could the ghost on Easton Street be that of the boy who drowned in the pit? Is it a boy who lost his family in a devastating house fire or a witness to the massive explosion that ripped Virgil McDonald to pieces? No one knows for sure, but the specters keep Owen Park a place of both beauty and intrigue.

The "Unknown House" in Owen Park

The strange and quirky structure in Owen Park known as the Unknown House has secrets hidden within its walls, or, more accurately, within its tunnels. There is supposedly a secret tunnel in the house once used by an Okie bootlegger.

The home was built in 1910 on 40 acres of land near Owen Park. With the growth of the Owen Park neighborhood, the land accompanying the Unknown House was reduced to three acres. The bizarre house has some features that are truly unusual. The living room is full of dark wood across the ceiling and walls, making the room mysterious, foreboding, and secretive. There is a now inactive gas pipe that once provided fuel for the living room chandelier that is as old as the house itself. A dining room that adjoins the living area has a built-in china cabinet with leaded glass, which was popular at the time it was constructed. It is definitely something that adds character to the home. Over the dining room table is the original chandelier that a former resident found in the basement coal chute cracked and nearly ruined. The resident carefully had the old fixture restored so it could shine on the evening meals once more. In the wood floor beneath the dining table is a small hole that raises a lot of questions. That hole once housed a button the owners used to call the servants to the table. Different renovations to the home have kept the house as close to its original state as possible and added both mystique and charm.

With a wraparound porch and cedar siding, the home is a true southern belle, but it also makes some strange noises. Residents of the house say they hear footsteps late at night as if someone is pacing the floors downstairs, but when they get up to check, nobody is there. There is a legend of a woman who suffered and died of tuberculosis inside the home and some speculate it could be her, lingering and unable to leave, or that it might be a loved one, worried about her deteriorating condition. Claims have been made that the old woman can be seen rocking in her chair on the large porch. Others assert seeing the rocking chair moving back and forth on its own.

There is much mystery attached to the Unknown House, with its false walls, hidden rooms, and concealed tunnels. Rumors those rooms and tunnels were used for illegal whiskey storage are probably not too far from the truth. The garage was utilized as a kitchen and carriage house in its former incarnation. Several decades ago, the upstairs kitchen caught on fire and caused severe damage to the home. There are many questions and speculation that the basement coal chute was once the tunnel's entry point, which could also be someplace else, hidden in the walls and secret rooms yet to be found. It is quite apparent the Unknown House has a murky past of veiled secrets and buried stories that will forever remain within its walls.

The Creepy House on Gilcrease Drive

The Gilcrease district of homes is located on a hill just north and west of downtown Tulsa. There is a legend about a house on Gilcrease Drive that seems to be a contributing factor to its vacancy. Neighbors say the house has been up for sale for years.

There is a story about a very controlling husband who kept his family hostage in the house, not allowing them any contact with the outside world. The legend continues that one day the man went crazy and killed the entire family before killing himself. It's said that on certain eerie nights, he can be seen roaming the front yard with a shotgun and looking angry and mean. Many claim to also see the faces of some very sad children looking out the window. Visitors to the house say it is creepy and has an "odd" feel. Claims have been made that the basement is like a jail cell, with huge metal doors, and that it is cold, damp, and forbidding.

The Deer Woman at Mohawk Park

The Tulsa parks system began over 100 years ago when early Native Americans came to Oklahoma. They settled in an area now known as Mohawk Park and used the land for powwows and other rituals; it was nearly considered sacred ground. Creek tribes were said to gather here for many purposes, and the majestic, mature trees that surround the park were said to talk to visitors. The aura of the land feels very sacred. Mohawk is one of Tulsa's oldest parks.

For years there have myths and legends about a Deer Woman in Mohawk Park. A Deer Woman is a creature in American Indian mythology also often referred to as a Deer Lady and known as a shape-shifter. She is part deer, part woman, and appears differently to various people. Sometimes she is seen as a young vixen and at other times she is an old lady. Legends say that the Deer Woman's primary role was to act as a siren and lure men to their deaths. She would hide partly behind a bush or tree and summon men to come to her. She is usually described as bare-breasted and beautiful, except for her hooves and large deer eyes. Her hooves are not noticeable to the man she beckons until it is too late. By the time he realizes she is not a normal woman, she tramples him to death or leads him over a cliff to his demise. The Deer Woman is said to be around not only Mohawk Park but also Grand Lake. She is believed to appear at stomp grounds during stomp ceremonies. The Seneca-Cayuga tribe has regular powwows at Grand Lake and has reported a young, attractive Native American girl attempting to coax men away. The legend of the Deer Woman is still alive and very well known in and around Tulsa. Men should be leery of a woman they see in the woods hiding behind a tree or bush as the Deer Woman could be calling for them.

There is a golf course that was added to Mohawk Park in the late 1920s that appears to have a nighttime phantom golfer. One of the old restroom facilities still located on the course is said to have an unknown visitor. Sometimes a light can be seen after dark on the women's side of the structure. But there is no electricity running to the building. It is also rumored that the vents in the women's room constantly emit cold air as if an air conditioner were on.

Nine

TULSA'S GHOSTLY SUBURBS

Broken Arrow, Oklahoma

Southeast of Tulsa is its largest suburb, Broken Arrow, or as most locals refer to it, BA. This fashionable little town boasts an estimated 90,000 or more residents today. Founded in 1902 by a Creek tribe that was moved to Oklahoma, the community was named after a creek in Alabama called Broken Arrow Creek, which is where the tribe had first settled. It is also said the name originated because the Creek Indians would break rather than cut branches off of trees to make their arrows.

After the Oklahoma town was established, land development had the help of services for a railroad that went through the town. Eventually, banks, dry goods stores, hotels, and other businesses began to spring up, and the economy thrived due to coal and agriculture industries. The first school was built in 1904, and this small town was quickly turning into a suburban city. On Tiger Hill in Broken Arrow is the place where Sylvester Morris, owner of Tulsa's oldest house, would preach sermons to crowds that would come from miles around to hear the good reverend speak.

BA remained a quiet little suburb that kept its distance from the disruption and chaos that

This unidentified Tulsa cabin is similar to others that housed some of the strange events that have peppered the city's past.

was taking place nearby in Tulsa. However, this popular town does have some secrets within its perimeters. While the town did not play an active role in the Tulsa Race Riots, it is rumored that a house in Broken Arrow once belonged to the Ku Klux Klan. Legends that the Klan would gather there and have bonfires into the night were plentiful, yet the little town remained silent when it came to acknowledging the terrible affair.

Today, economic development has turned this small town into one that is referred to as Tulsa's fastest growing and most desirable suburb. Victorian homes that decorate the historic downtown and complement other buildings in the district tell of a time when roosters were sold on Main Street and large festivals filled the streets with commerce and hospitable citizens.

Broken Arrow has earned the reputation of being Oklahoma's safest city several years in a row. However, it appears that the town is not safe from the legends and tales of a time that left a ghostly impression on this beautiful town.

The "Devil House"

Today the concrete house that once belonged to the KKK is gone, built over or never existing in the first place. Spectral rumors, however, flood the area where the house is said to have once stood. In most descriptions, the old, abandoned, condemned structure now referred to as the Devil House stood on a single dirt road in the middle of nowhere. The land where the house is said to have existed is the sight of disappearing bonfires, oddly cold temperatures, and a speeding car that is said to make a very sharp turn and disappear through a barbed wire fence into a cornfield. When the car is seen by witnesses, there is no obvious disturbance of the dirt or gravel, and no tire tracks or other signs of the car's speedy passage. Some believe the car contained some kids who would watch the Klan in hopes of one day being a member but when caught, were chased away and killed in a fiery crash.

Nazi POW Camp

Another area of interest in Broken Arrow is said to have once been a German prisoner-of-war camp just north of the Aransas River. There is an old military installation that has been vacant, abandoned, and shut down for years but rumors that it once held Nazi prisoners from World War II are still being told today. Legend says that late at night odd noises can be heard coming from the property and that walking up to the gate makes a person ill, sick to their stomach with a feeling of unshakable misery overcoming them.

Tulsa's Haunted Memories

Baker Oil Tools

Located in the heart of Broken Arrow is the popular Baker Oil Tools, renowned for making oil field equipment. There is a rumor that a former worker lost his life in a freak accident on the second floor of the building, and some say they can hear a man moaning, while others refuse to go upstairs because it is so spooky. Legend says that the former employee still roams the upper floor of this business and is especially active at night.

Haikey Creek

Located on 151 acres providing picnic shelters, disc golf, grills, baseball fields, and playground equipment is a picturesque park known as Haikey Creek. Along Haikey Creek are jogging and walking trails that wander into the woods and benches and other recreational items for visitors to enjoy. There is a rumor that a man was driving too fast through the area once on his motorcycle, wrecked, and met a sudden death. Sightings of a man emerging from the woods with a very large bloody gash on his head who causes unsuspecting passers to feel quite uncomfortable when they ask him if he needs help and he disappears have been reported along the walking trail. Many accounts of the vanishing wreck victim have been reported in the Haikey Creek area and continue to haunt the beautiful area.

Pryor, Oklahoma

Just northeast of Tulsa stands the old "war boom" town of Pryor, Oklahoma. Originally known as Pryor Creek, this rural community was established in 1820 as early pioneers traveled through the area. Capt. Nathaniel Pryor settled and established the first trading post on Grand River around the time the Perrymans were doing the same in Tulsa. Captain Pryor had been a member of the Lewis and Clark Expedition.

The town of Pryor was pretty much desolate until it came to life in 1870 with the construction of the railroad that would eventually bring business and commerce. The post office established the town name as "Coo-y-yah" which was Cherokee for huckleberry. In 1887, the town name was changed to Pryor Creek due to white men's inability to spell and pronounce the Native American language correctly. Later the town dropped the word Creek from its name and was simply referred to as Pryor, although official city documents still call the town Pryor Creek.

Today, Pryor has a population of about 8,500 people and is mostly known for it large agricultural economy. Beef cattle and cash crops built the city of Pryor, and it is widely known for its horse and dairy industries. The enigmatic little town is said to have some very diverse and interesting people, both living and not living. Being over 185 years old, this town is bound to be home to many ghosts. It is not surprising considering the devastation the small community witnessed one spring afternoon.

It was in April 1942, just after the town and country had overcome the Great Depression, when a disaster destroyed Pryor. It was around 4:45 in the afternoon, according to the post office clock that stopped working, when dark and ominous clouds were approaching the city from the west. Many believed the dark clouds to be nothing more than a famous Oklahoma thunderstorm. What they got instead would forever haunt the city and its people. Indeed a storm was approaching, and while some folks began to take shelter, others went about their daily business. A tornado, now estimated to be F4 strength, had touched down in Rogers County killing three people in Talala, Oklahoma, and was heading straight for downtown Pryor. The town did not have a tornado warning system in place at that time, and as black funnel clouds began to swirl over the city, a threatening tone was being set along Highway 20 where the cyclone was traveling. The funnel cloud eventually touched down, and the twister headed straight down Main Street, destroying buildings and houses and ripping the town to shreds. Debris and bodies were flying through the sky as the tornado danced through the streets, swaying back and forth through the populated business district. The two-block-wide path of the storm stopped dead at the city cemetery and rose back into the sky, but not before ripping off the top of the water tower that stood right beside it. Heavy rains following the storm, causing massive flooding to the city, and people were running through the streets in panic and chaos. The destructive tornado seriously injured over 450 people and killed more than 50. Downtown businesses and homes were leveled, and the two main hospitals in the town were destroyed. The estimated damage was over $2 million. A few places to the town's north that were untouched by the storm needed power, and people from nearby towns came with generators to help until the Red Cross and emergency services could get there. A small house that was renovated into a private doctor's clinic was made into a makeshift hospital, and the First Christian Church served as a temporary morgue. Thunderbird Academy, a military operation for youths, was also used as a temporary hospital. The *Pryor Daily Democrat* reported that bodies were being found in creek bottoms and ravines, and the sounds of ambulance screams filled the night as townspeople in shock wandered aimlessly through the streets looking at Mother Nature's wrath.

While it is reported that many of the downtown buildings were rebuilt, most of them went to one-story structures from the two and three stories they once were. It was obvious the town of Pryor would never be the same. Was the storm and the deaths it caused the reason for the many ghostly stories that come from Pryor? No one knows for sure, but one thing is certain: many claim that a creepy feeling comes over them when they enter the little town.

TULSA'S HAUNTED MEMORIES

Moots Hospital

A small 25-bed hospital facility was founded by Dr. Glen Moots. Built sometime in the 1930s, the hospital was said to be haunted. The building took the brunt of the 1942 tornado and sat vacant for many years. People claimed they could detect movement from inside the building. Echoes of machines and voices were said to be heard bouncing off the torn walls of the structure. It was one of only two hospitals in Pryor, and it was not rebuilt after the tornado. The property was up for sale for years and the old shell that remained was eventually torn down and is but a memory today.

Phantom Hitchhiker

Driving along Highway 20 just east of Claremore, drivers sometimes find themselves with unexpected company. It was the winter of 1965 when a woman named Mae Doria noticed a young boy hitchhiking along the side of the road. She offered the boy a ride, and he sat quietly in the back seat of her car until they approached the town of Pryor. As they were driving into the town, the boy asked to be let out of the car in an area where there were no houses around. Confused, Doria asked the boy where he lived, but he simply replied "over there." She turned to look and see what he meant, and when she turned around to ask him again, he was gone. Doria immediately got out of the car, looked around, and called out for him, but the child had seemed to simply vanish into thin air. Two years later, Doria was talking to a man about her strange experience with the disappearing hitchhiker. He knew immediately where she was talking about. He had heard about the phantom hitchhiker being picked up along Highway 20 since 1936. No one knows the boy's name, his purpose, or what happened to him, but those who have encountered him say he is very real. There are still reports today of the phantom hitchhiker that haunts Highway 20, and it seems the boy has made himself a legend along the stretch of lonely highway.

Thunderbird Academy

Once a state-owned orphanage, Thunderbird Youth Academy started as Whitaker Indian Orphanage, founded by Mr. and Mrs. W. T. Whitaker in 1881 on 40 acres of land. After the Civil War, there was a large number of children who were left abandoned after surviving their parents. Eventually, the Whitaker Orphanage took in those children and became the Whitaker Children's Home. At that time, the shortage of schools for non-Indian children made it necessary for the Whitakers to provide not only shelter, clothing, and food, but also classroom and training facilities. With this growth, the property grew to 590 acres and went from a one-home structure to over 30 buildings. It included a farm and was mostly self-sufficient, raising its own hogs, beef, and dairy to provide for its needs. The children learned discipline and teamwork as they shared the workload and provided for their brothers and sisters. As the children grew up and left the facility, it was apparent the Whitakers had done a fantastic job, as these well-adjusted individuals became productive members of society.

There is a small cemetery on the property that is the resting place of children who died while residing at the home. The original tombstone is still there but is very worn from the weather. The tombstone was a commemorative marker with the names and dates of the children it honored. The people of Pryor eventually copied the entries and had a new stone erected in a nearby location.

In 1908, the orphanage was taken over by the State of Oklahoma and operated as a home for neglected and dependent children for several years. Today, it is the site of a military school for troubled youth known as Thunderbird Youth Academy.

The story says that some of the cadets are awakened at night to the sound of children talking and laughing. Witnesses have claimed that a child haunts the attic of what is now the Third Platoon Building. Apparitions and noises are said to be heard through the buildings at Thunderbird. Since the place's history is not one of tragedy but rather one of hope, it makes little sense that the place would be haunted, but the stories that continue to come from Thunderbird make it difficult to deny. The facility was used as a makeshift hospital during the 1942 tornado, and many assume that the lives lost are still lingering there as well as the children who perished during their short stays at the orphanage.

Main Street

Multiple lives were lost in the 1942 tornado, and many downtown businesses claim strange activity and spectral sightings because of it. A pool hall that once sat along Main Street was said to have a lot of ghostly activity. Billiard balls were witnessed moving on their own and being picked up and thrown across the room as if on their own. Other claims of poltergeist activity have been reported there as well.

An old funeral home situated off of Main Street is said to have reported strange activity such as growls and noises as well as apparitions and shadowy figures that are seen at any given moment they choose to show themselves.

Sightings of Bigfoot, or Sasquatch, have been reported in the wooded areas surrounding Pryor along with claims that bad things happen at a place called Robbers Canyon, said to exist on a private piece of land where outlaws are buried. A little girl around eight years old has been seen roaming the street and homes along 480 Road and has been referred to as the 480 Devil. She will suddenly appear, soaking wet, with a look in her eye that makes one not want to get close to her.

Many stories that come out of Pryor make the small town seem even smaller when the occupants who are said to be seen and then disappear without a trace are accounted for. It is thought those residents of Pryor keep the town interesting and mysterious.

Catoosa, Oklahoma

Catoosa, Oklahoma, is 14 miles northeast of Tulsa. The first settlers are said to have made their homes here in 1839. This land was controlled by the Cherokee Nation until 1882 and lies along historic Route 66. The name Catoosa derives from Cherokee and means "new settlement place" or "on the hill." When the railroad came through and laid new tracks, Catoosa became a popular cow town and was widely known as a place to ship cattle east. In 1883, a post office was established, and the little cow town to the east was growing. It was shortly after the early 1900s when Catoosa began producing natural gas and petroleum. Agriculture and mining also played a role in giving the city of Catoosa its first breaths, and the city was off to making its mark on the state. Most notably in Catoosa is the inland seaport, the Port of Catoosa. It is the farthest inland seaport in the United States. Today Catoosa is known for many things, including one of the most recognized and famous roadside icons on Route 66, the large Blue Whale. However, Catoosa is also known for some strange and uninviting events as well, and there appear to be a number of them.

Redbud Valley

Redbud Valley is approximately 3.5 miles north of Interstate 44 on 161st East Avenue. Its beautiful nature preserve was said to have been a regular hideout for the Doolin-Dalton gang when they came through Tulsa on their crime sprees.

Back in 1976, this was the site of a very unfortunate incident with a young schoolgirl. Her name was Karla and her body was found near a bridge a few days after she had been brutally murdered. The bridge gained the nickname of "Karla's Bridge," and the sound of a young girl laughing and crying has been reported at this location.

Another tale of Redbud Valley involves claims of a fire seen atop a hill that disappears when someone tries to find it. Some claim the weird image is not a fire at all but in fact an orange ball of light. Reports of seeing it on the hill and near the bridge are common. People have described the image as emergency vehicle lights coming over the hill only to get near it before it disappears.

The road that travels through Redbud Valley has a cryptic history. Several serious auto accidents have occurred on the road at the small bridge. The local sheriff's department has said it was the most dangerous road in the county for fatalities. With the numerous sightings reported here, it does leave questions of who is involved and why this is happening in this area. For now, it will continue to remain a mystery.

Dick Duck Cemetery

Yes, that is the real name of a cemetery located East of Tulsa off 193rd East Avenue at Pine Street. A very old cemetery dating back to the 1830s, it was named after Richard "Dick" Duck, an Indian who donated the land, which was already serving as a graveyard. The burial ground consists of many old settlers who died from various diseases or murders by gangs. There are two very old Indian stone grave houses on the site, and the first burial was said to be that of Bonnie Smith in 1834.

One of the most famous outlaws buried at Dick Duck Cemetery is that of Bluford "Blue" Duck. He was born in the Cherokee Nation and was a member of a gang that participated in stage hold-ups and rustling. Sometime in the 1870s, it was said that Bluford had a short affair with gang member and outlaw Belle Starr. Several years later she met and married Sam Starr, and a new gang was formed They were notorious for stealing horses, bootlegging whiskey to Indians, and cattle rustling, and it was rumored that Bluford "Blue" Duck joined them quite often on their crime sprees.

In June 1884, Bluford and a friend named William Christie were drunk and riding their horses through Indian Territory causing a ruckus. While passing through the Cherokee Nation, they came upon a farmer working in his field. This young farmer was known as Samuel Wyrick. As the pair rode up to him, Bluford Duck retrieved his gun and unloaded it on the unsuspecting farmer. He reloaded the gun and then shot a young Indian boy who was helping and shot the horse the boy was sitting on as well. No one knows the reason for the senseless crime, but Duck and Christie were sentenced to death. In July 1886, Duck was sentenced to hang for the murders. The charges against William Christie were dropped, and he was set free.

Belle Starr's efforts to help Blue Duck in his appeals to be spared the hanging sentence were successful, and Duck's punishment was changed to life in prison. In 1895, he became deathly ill with tuberculosis and was given just one month to live. President Cleveland pardoned him, and Duck was sent home with family and friends. Bluford "Blue" Duck died on May 7, 1895, and is buried in Dick Duck Cemetery today.

Many claim it is Blue Duck who haunts the cemetery. Reports of a strange Indian language and other noises and ghostly phenomena are common at Dick Duck Cemetery. Several visitors claim that an eerie feeling comes over them when they drive past or enter the rickety chain-link fence. There are also several unmarked graves of children who died of tuberculosis and other diseases. Those children are said to be seen and heard at the cemetery at night. With such a history, this cemetery no doubt has some hidden stories.

Tulsa's Haunted Memories

Sapulpa, Oklahoma

Just 15 miles southwest of Tulsa is a little town named after a young Creek Indian known as Sapulpa. He moved to Indian Territory in 1840, when many others were settling into the land after the Trail of Tears. Chief Sapulpa was a full-blood Creek who arrived in Tulsa from Alabama, where he was a member of the Kasihta tribe. He served in the Confederate army in the Civil War and was also a rancher. Sapulpa established the first trading post and was the first occupant of this Tulsa suburb.

When the railroad was building through Indian Territory in the 1880s, it came through Sapulpa. The chief is said to have befriended the railway workers, and they called his little village Sapulpa Station. In 1889, a post office was established and Sapulpa was becoming known as a town. With the glass plants and other manufacturing facilities taking up residence in Sapulpa, what was once a sleepy little village had become a bustling community.

Haunted Fire Station

In Sapulpa, there is an old fire station located at 123 East Hobson Street. An ambulance company later took over the building, but before it was the fire station, it was said to have been the site of an old jailhouse. When they were alone in the building, workers would claim to see dark apparitions in the ambulance bays.

The presence of ghostly images is said to haunt the bay due to former inmates who were killed or committed suicide by hanging themselves. Workers at the building claimed they could feel a strong, intimidating presence. When the ambulance bays were empty because both vehicles had been dispatched is when paranormal activity was alleged to be at its strongest, most apparent level.

South Heights

There is a cemetery in Sapulpa known as South Heights. It is a very old graveyard located just off Mission Street at the corner of Line Street. The first documented burial at the cemetery was in 1920, but some early settlers are said to be buried here, dating back to the late 1800s. It seems that many times emergency medical services and the Sapulpa Police Department have been called out to the area due to sightings of people entering the mausoleum after dark. When police and emergency personnel investigate, the structure is found empty yet calls continue to pour in even while officer sand paramedics are still at the site looking for the alleged trespassers. It is said the police have even witnessed people walking into the mausoleum, and as officers followed them in to question them about why they were there, the crypt would be found empty. No one knows who it is that is seen entering the mausoleum after dark, but many agree that whoever it is appears to be very elusive and crafty at disappearing once he is seen entering.

The Unknown Soldier

Many have reported seeing a man in an armed forces uniform marching on Sapulpa Street but then mysteriously disappearing. Residents claim that every so often when he is seen, he appears to be on a mission.

Biven Creek

There is also a former watering hole now known as Biven Creek. It is rumored the area is haunted by a woman who throws rocks and bricks into the creek. People who have seen her describe her as being badly burned and wearing long hair and shabby clothes. Some say she is the victim of an old car crash years ago, yet others tell a different story. Some of the local Sapulpa residents believe she is a witch who was burned and still curses the property in retribution. Whatever the case, those who have witnessed the woman claim she is in a trancelike state and not someone they wish to approach. Some have called the woman evil, and others have called her sad; but whoever she is, her spirit remains along the banks of Biven Creek. The mystery that surrounds her is one that is both haunting and fascinating.

Sand Springs, Oklahoma

The earliest recorded settlement of Sand Springs was in 1826. Creek Indians who relocated to the land during the Trail of Tears made Sand Springs their home. The first settler was said to have been Governor Lieutenant Adams, a Confederate Indian who brought his family to the area and took up residence by a natural spring. This is how Sand Springs was said to have acquired its name. The town was originally known as Adam Springs, but the name was later changed. As white settlers moved into the area, they forced the Creek Indians out of their land. The Creeks left Sand Springs abruptly, taking everything with them except the burial ground that is still there today.

In 1908, wealthy oilman Charles Page purchased 126 acres of land with the intent of building an orphanage. The orphanage started in a tent with seven homeless children, and a permanent structure was built in 1917 to accommodate up to 75 children. Cottages were also built as shelter for homeless mothers and their children. Charles Page did a lot for the city of Sand Springs with

Exit Adams Road in Sand Springs, Oklahoma, and you will find an old Indian burial ground. Seen here in 1883, the Tullahassee Creek Indian Cemetery, also known as the Adams Creek Cemetery, had mainly Adams family Creek Indians buried there. The last burial was in 1912. The Adams Creek Cemetery is still there today but it is fenced off and located in the middle of a strip mall parking lot.

his discovery of natural gas. His drilling led to abundant amounts of fuel found in the Tulsa earth. This discovery made the town one of industry and manufacturing, and it continued to grow—as did Page's generosity.

Not only was Sand Springs gaining a reputation as the leading industrial city in the state, but it was also known for the caring and close-knit community it had become. A number of institutions were built to help its citizens. The Sand Springs home for widows and children was established, as was the Salvation Army Maternity Home and the Sand Springs School for the Deaf. Those less fortunate found solace in the town of Sand Springs.

Bulldog Man

One example of that compassion is the famous legend of the Bulldog Man. The story goes that in the 1920s on the northern border of town, there was a street that wound though Tulsa and into Sand Springs. The street was known as Old North Road and at the bend in the road there once stood an amusement park said to be the equivalent of Coney Island. People from all over the country would visit the park, bringing their families there for vacations and getaways. It was said to be a Disneyland or Six Flags of the 1920s and quite a popular place to visit.

Myths of the area say that one very poor family was driving by the park but had too many children and could not afford to enter. The family watched all the fun going on inside from the parking lot. Rumors say they either forgot or abandoned one of their young boys and left him behind. The boy lived off discarded food while hiding in the park at night. When a couple of years later the park was closed down, the boy found himself wandering around the woods surrounding the site when he came across a brick factory. He wandered inside and found a warm spot next to some freshly baked bricks that gave him warmth in the cool evenings. One night a pile of bricks that was cooling shifted and fell on the boy, disfiguring his face to the point where he looked like a bulldog. It is said he had a pug nose and hanging jowls and so the factory workers nicknamed him Bulldog Boy. They could not afford to get medical attention for him, but his face did heal, although a bit flawed from the accident. The workers at the factory adopted the boy, bringing him food and allowing him to stay in and around the brickyard.

The boy grew up with the brickyard workers, expecting to get a job at the factory when he got older, but the factory closed down before that happened. The mutilated and uneducated minor learned to live off the land. By the time he turned 17, the boy had become accustomed to being antisocial and lived as a hermit in a worn-down shack in the woods off of Old North Road. It was said that he would shoot at anyone and anything that came near him in fear of what people would think about his appearance. He ate discarded hot dogs, hamburgers, and fries that local kids would throw out of their car windows at a place on Old North Road known as a hangout for partying and making out. Legend says the Bulldog Man survived for years this way while guarding the brickyard he knew as home. Rumors surfaced that the Bulldog Man would intentionally come out and scare kids if they did not leave food behind. Today the area surrounding Old North Road has been developed, and the brickyard has since been bulldozed. Where there was once a thriving amusement park and a brickyard, there is now an upscale nursing home.

There is also a second story regarding the Bulldog Man that dates back to the 1850s. Legend says that a man was working late at the brick factory one evening when there was a sudden explosion. His face was extremely disfigured in the accident, but he did survive. It is said that he could no longer take the whispers, stares, and giggles that people made, and so he retreated to the woods for a life of solitude.

Whatever happened to the Bulldog Man no one knows, but kids still claim sightings and glimpses of him tromping through the woods. Many do not know if it is the ghost of the Bulldog Man or actually him, in what would now be his elderly years. Whatever the case, the legend of Bulldog Man is still alive and well in Sand Springs.

Charles Page High School

Named after the wealthy oilman and founder of Sand Springs, Charles Page High School on Adams Road is the home of the Sandites and, allegedly, a few ghosts.

The high school was built in 1959, and it is rumored that during construction a terrible accident occurred. The roof of the building collapsed on a worker, causing him to fall 60 feet to his death. It was a tragic day and a very sudden, unexpected death. Some claim that the construction worker continues to haunt the school. Whoever it is, he is causing quite a few disturbances in the auditorium. Strange sounds, lights, and voices have kept some students from ever setting foot in the auditorium.

It was said to have started in the early 1970s, when a green light in the balcony area would refuse to go off. Even with the manipulation of the breaker, the light would stay on. Voices are heard in the auditorium quite regularly. Usually the voices are muffled, making it hard to distinguish the dialogue. However, many witnesses say it sounds like an argument that suddenly stops and disappears. In fact, an alarm company called the principal one evening and told him the voices in the auditorium were so loud they would have to turn off the monitor in order to watch the rest of the school. The ruckus coming from the empty auditorium was so disturbing that the alarm company did turn off the monitor to that room. Witnesses have included students and faculty alike. Once while a boy was looking at the stage, he and his teacher noticed a light go zooming through the stage area. The boy jumped, and the teacher asked the student if he just saw the same thing. The two concurred they had both seen something strange and could not account for it.

So many unusual things have happened in the auditorium, it is certain that someone or something is causing the commotion. An entire class, students and their teacher, once witnessed the ghost firsthand. As the students were quietly sitting in the auditorium listening to the teacher give his lesson, the lights began to dim. Soon they began to flicker several times and go off. The lights would come back on, but a few moments later they would again begin to dim, flicker, and go off. This happened several times, sparking nervous laughter from the students. It was obviously becoming uncomfortable for them as they were showing signs of uneasiness in their faces and behavior. The teacher could not teach because of the interruptions and asked aloud for the lights to stay on because they were having class. At that moment, the lights came back on and never dimmed or flickered again. It seems someone surely wants to make his presence known.

Cry Baby Bridge

Of course, no city is complete without its "Cry Baby Bridge." While this legend seems to be in many different cities around the nation, many believe it stems from an actual event, but where it originated remains a mystery. Sand Springs claims to have its own version of this infamous and legendary bridge. Northwest of the city is Shell Creek Bridge, which is said to be the home of a crying baby. Rumors that a bad car accident happened on this bridge and a mother and baby drowned have haunted the area for decades. Visitors to the bridge claim that late at night they can hear the faint cry of the baby who was killed in that fatal car wreck.

Page Memorial Cemetery

In this old cemetery, people visiting will see names on tombstones of people they know to be alive. When they inquire with the cemetery staff, there is no record of such a person being buried there. When they return to show the headstone to the caretaker, either they cannot find it or the area in which they saw it will be an empty plot.

Garfield Street

Many residents growing up on or around Garfield Street and across from the cemetery have reported strange happenings in their homes. Homeowners have claimed to hear children playing or young children running through the house. Those residents with children would swear they would hear the sounds when their child was not at home or was asleep. People also claimed their children would talk about "playing with the kids" and make comments about children who were not there. Whispers and whistles are another common sound heard among the homes on Garfield Street.

Tulsa's Haunted Memories

Overlook Drive

There is an ominous stretch of road off Highway 97 just past the golf course. Locals know it as Overlook Drive. On rainy nights, drivers are said to see a shadow on the side of the road that will strangely disappear as they approach it. The few who have gotten a glimpse of the dark stranger say it is a man wearing a black hoodie and jeans. As they continue past the area and look back in disbelief, they will see the same dark figure lying in the road behind them.

Ten

HAUNTED GREEN COUNTRY

Green Country is the entire northeast corner of the state from I-40 North to I-35 East. Tulsa lies within the Green Country boundary, and this area has some freaky history and the urban legends that accompany it. Most of the places mentioned are but a short drive from Tulsa, and the stories have haunted the area for years.

New Prue / Old Prue

Located in Osage County in the Tulsa metropolitan area is a little stretch of land no longer than a mile that is known as the town of New Prue. The reason for the "New" in its name is because the old town is now under water. When construction began on the Keystone Dam in 1964, the town of Prue moved permanently, and the old town was covered with water. This body of water is called Lake Keystone, a very popular hangout during the blistering Tulsa summer months. Visitors to the lake claim they can sometimes see lights coming on in buildings underneath the water. Reports of flashing and moving lights have been witnessed as well as ghostly figures and shadowy apparitions seen along the shore. The strange underwater anomalies keep the visitors to the lake wondering what is happening in Old Prue.

Shawnee, Oklahoma

Shawnee is a small bedroom community that was not officially settled until after the Civil War. When Indians were moved to Oklahoma by the government, Shawnee started to come to life. Soon schools, railroads, commercial buildings, and missions were a part of the community. With the pressure of commerce, Shawnee would soon see white settlers move in. Known for its agricultural business with cotton and peaches, this southern Oklahoma town saw its main street lined up with mule sellers, peanut vendors, and peach growers from nearby cities. Like many Oklahoma communities, it benefited from the oil boom of the 1920s and saw significant growth. While the history of Shawnee is rather benign, its ghostly specters are not. Could it be because so many of the buildings on Main Street are original and untouched? Walking into a business on the street or simply driving down it is almost like stepping back in time. The charm and nostalgia of Shawnee is still alive and well. . . . as are its specters.

St. Gregory's University

Founded in October of 1875 by two French monks who were wandering across Indian Territory, St. Gregory's University was created to minister to and educate early settlers about the Roman Catholic doctrine and practices. The monks started their mission in a little town called Konawa and established a church, convent, school, boys' home, and three-story monastery on Bald Hill. They continued to build the mission for the next 25 years, adding the renowned St. Gregory's College. They were growing their vision of higher education and Catholic values.

In a devastating fire in 1901, the buildings were destroyed. While some were rebuilt, others were not, and so the school was moved permanently to Shawnee. All that remains are empty building foundations, abandoned memories of a time when the cradle of Oklahoma Catholicism was active. What do remain are three different Sacred Heart cemeteries that are the final resting place of monks, Indians, and early settlers. People brave enough to go inside have reported the cemeteries to be extremely haunted.

The St. Gregory's building was constructed in Shawnee in the late 1940s, and nothing tragic has ever been associated with it, but with so much left behind at the old site at Sacred Heart, many believe the spirits have followed the mission for that purpose. Alumni of the school say the monks are very open and willing to discuss the odd happenings that some of the students were experiencing. The Roman Catholic faith is one of the only Christian denominations that acknowledges and accepts the possibility of paranormal and ghostly activity. It was even said the monks were amused by the stories they were told.

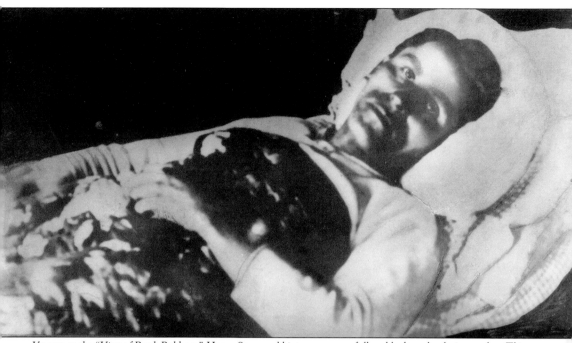

Known as the "King of Bank Robbers," Henry Starr and his posse successfully robbed two banks in one day. This robbery was the first of its kind accomplished by a band of outlaws in the United States. The picture above was taken just minutes after Starr was shot by Paul Quarry on March 27, 1915, in Stroud, Oklahoma.

One legend tells of a student who fell asleep in the library one evening while doing a research paper. He was awakened by a monk who very kindheartedly helped him find books that he would need to complete his paper. The monk then helped the student out of the library and back to his dorm. When the student returned the books to the library, it was found out the monk who had helped him that evening had died over 10 years earlier.

It is no secret around St. Gregory's University that the ghosts of the past still roam the college and grounds. Another story from a dorm mother said that one summer she was helping the brothers and other university staff paint the girls' rooms. As everyone was leaving, the matron was on the first floor gathering her belongings to leave when she heard the slamming of doors from the third floor. The slamming continued, one after another, with a very loud slam of each door one at a time. After the noise reached the second floor, whatever it was began to slam the doors in succession all the way to the first floor and next to the room where the matron was standing. Needless to say, the intense experience sent the dorm mother quickly exiting the building.

Legend says that old monks from long ago still roam the buildings, corridors, and grounds of the prestigious university. Animals making odd noises and appearing in and disappearing into thin air have been reported. A statue of a woman that stands in front of the church was said to be heard crying and moaning. Other rumors say that a mist has been seen roaming across the cemeteries and that an old lady has been seen walking with a panther. It seems the claims of Sacred Heart are plenty and even include Civil War soldiers and sightings of a flame next to a witch who was burned at the stake. Whoever takes up ghostly residence with the staff and faculty are not shy in making sure that the curriculum is followed, that students get the help they need, and that visitors do not wear out their welcome.

Walls Bargain Center

While it is true that shoppers can get a bargain at Walls Bargain Center, they can also get more than they bargained for! It seems that there is a ghost who wanders the aisles of the store, and many employees will declare that the store is downright creepy at times.

Employees have long told of how they would arrive to open in the mornings and find the store in disarray. They would discover merchandise strewn across the floor when no one had been inside the building to cause it. They would also complain of strange noises they would hear in the back storage room that resembled the flapping sound from the double doors, but the problem was that no one was back there. Unable to explain the phenomena, they could only chalk it up to that strange fellow several employees have seen randomly around the place.

Several workers have witnessed an apparition of a man dressed in gray wandering the store and then disappearing. They have given him the nickname Charlie, and they believe he is the culprit behind the strange and unusual things that happen inside the store when it is locked up for the night.

While Charlie is still somewhat of a mystery, there is a legend from long ago of a man who was shot and broke into the store to hide. He went to the second story, where he collapsed and bled to death. No one knows who Charlie is or where he has come from, but one thing is for sure: the mysterious man is one who likes to make sure the employees have plenty of work.

The Search House

The Search House is a striking mansion built in 1901. The land where the house was constructed was from the original Beard land grant and owned by a rich banker. The property was later donated to the railroad in an attempt to bring more business to the city of Shawnee. The home has been rumored to have once been used as a boardinghouse. It still has as much charm today as it did back then, with original stained glass windows, hardware, spacious rooms, and tall ceilings. The 3,300-square-foot home has five very large bedrooms and two full bathrooms. It has a formal parlor, dining room, and living room, as well as a breakfast nook. The basement was converted into a one-bedroom apartment and has its own kitchen and bathroom as well as a private outside entrance. In addition, there is a one-bedroom cottage behind the house that is said to have been the servant quarters at one time.

While the history of the house is rather mild, the ghostly activity is not. The Search House is rumored to be the home of several ghosts—from an older gentleman to a pair of small children. Closet doors open by themselves, and knobs have been seen to jiggle as if someone were trying to open the door. Footsteps have been heard on the stairwell and in the upstairs hallways, and bare footprints of a child were found on the wet paint of a bedroom door that was lying on the floor to dry. Giggling and the sound of small feet running through the house have startled guests, owners, and visitors to the Search House.

One ghost is referred to as Mr. George and has been seen throughout the mansion quite often. Some believe it to be a former owner, and others believe he is a relative of a former owner. Whatever the case, the apparitions that have been seen at this old house lead some to claim it is extremely haunted.

Guthrie, Oklahoma

The small town along I-35 and just north of Oklahoma City known as Guthrie was originally Oklahoma's capital. The sound of a cannon and the pounding of horse hooves in 1889 found 10,000 people clamoring to settle in Guthrie. In only a few months, the city's population had surpassed that of some of the more sophisticated and established cities on the east coast. Guthrie soon had running water, electricity, and underground garages for carriages as well as brick and stone buildings boasting a modern way of life. The city also developed a transit system and was booming with notoriety.

It was named Oklahoma's state capital in 1907, just after statehood, but a political scandal and commotion moved the state seat to Oklahoma City in 1910. Oklahoma City becoming the seat of state government took commerce with it, causing the town of Guthrie to go into an economic hibernation for nearly 70 years. Guthrie is a quiet, sleepy little town that has some amazing restored buildings that reflect the grandeur that once made it a viable candidate to be the state capital. It also has some rather unusual places among its neighborhoods that only add to its character.

The Stone Lion Inn

The old Victorian mansion in Guthrie known as the Stone Lion Inn was built in 1907. It served as a private residence to the F. E. Houghton family. Having a rather large family with 10 children, Houghton built the 8,000-square-foot, four-story home. The final cost was $11,900, a small price to pay for the welfare and comfort of his family, even back then. Two stone lions flank the steps leading to its front door as a symbol of protection and elegance.

One of the legends that accompany the house is about the Houghtons' daughter Augusta. Inaccurate tales of her ghost haunting the inn were plentiful when it was rumored she died of whooping cough. It was said she was administered too much medicine from the maid and so she haunted the house in retribution. However, historical research has proved that Augusta was still alive, but another daughter who died of whooping cough under the same circumstances could be the child haunting the place. Whoever it is, the spirit has left no doubts in the minds of those who have spent time at the inn that something is there. Something is clearly lurking in the corners, halls, and rooms of the mysterious mansion. Visitors and staff alike will attest to the strange activity that happens at the century-old inn.

During the 1920s, the house was known as the Smith Funeral Home. Today the original embalming table is proudly displayed in the entryway as a table for cookies, flowers, and refreshments. For several years after the funeral home closed, the house remained abandoned and empty. The lonely house on Warner Avenue was a far cry from the days when children were laughing, running, and giggling through its halls. Its current owner purchased the dwelling in 1986, and renovations were carefully done to bring back the original grandeur. Since the purchase by the current owner, a record number of strange occurrences have been said to occur there.

A group of visitors came to the home because of their interest in the house's history. They were given permission to explore and found themselves in the attic. The attic had a low ceiling, and while it felt enclosed, it was a rather large oblong room. Windows that lined the walls had small pocket seats in front of them. Two of the visitors sat in one of the window seats and admired some pictures that were leaning against the wall, apparently being stored there. The two visitors got up from their spot, and when they returned to finish examining the pictures, a dead blackbird was lying in the window seat where they had just been sitting. Two other people were with them and on the opposite side of the attic, giving no explanation as to how the dead bird got there as all windows were closed. The bird had very little odor but appeared to have been dead for a while and was lying right where one of the visitors had just been sitting.

Other strange phenomena have been reported from the house, such as odd noises, smells, and voices. One visitor to the home told of a time when she was locked in the foyer restroom and could not get out. The visitor said that when she tried to leave the door would not unlock. She tried several times to get out, even pounding on the door to get someone's attention but to no avail. As frustration and panic began to set in, the door lock made a noise, moved, and seemingly unlocked itself. The visitor was finally free to leave the restroom, which she did with much haste.

Whatever or whoever is haunting the charming Stone Lion Inn in Guthrie, visitors to the Bed and Breakfast will have to take note of what is around them . . . especially where the foyer bathroom is located.

The Masonic Boys Home

Built in the 1920s, this old three-story house was used as a place for unfortunate orphaned children. Boys from all over the state were sent here to be cared for while waiting on adoption from a loving family.

One of the head matrons of the boy's home was said to be an overly strict woman who would frequently punish the boys in the most disturbing ways. Rumor says that one night while punishing a six-year-old boy, she killed him, and in fear of being caught, buried him in the basement of the home. The matron did not want to be hanged, which was the punishment for such a crime in those days. For several months, she got away with her dirty deed. While under great suspicion, she maintained her story that the boy ran away while being punished. She then used the excuse of putting the boys in the basement when they misbehaved to keep them from running away. Over the course of several years, the woman became notorious for using the basement as a lock-up for boys who needed discipline. The basement was an ideal place to punish the boys as no one could hear them scream for help as she administered her reprimand. Over the years, a few other boys mysteriously came up missing from the home and the matron would stand by her oath that they had run away. During routine maintenance of the house the matron would never allow access to the basement until there was a major plumbing problem that would force them to dig in the area. The night before, fearing what could be found out, the matron dug up the bones in the basement in an attempt to move them to another location. The janitor, who was extremely suspicious of her frequent visits to the basement, followed her and witnessed her digging up the bones and decayed corpses of the young boys. The janitor called the authorities, but the matron committed suicide before they arrived to avoid justice for her misdeeds. An investigation was initiated and concluded that the matron had indeed murdered five boys. The boy's home was shut down sometime in the 1930s and remained vacant for many years. During the Depression, the Freemasons purchased the building, but nothing was done with the structure and it remained abandoned and lonely.

There is another rumor about the building that has followed Guthrie citizens since statehood. It was said that a worker who knew about the murders committed by the head matron committed suicide in the bell tower after a dreadful bout of guilt. Claims that footsteps can be heard on the stairwell leading to the bell tower and heavy walking in the tower itself have been told for decades. Sightings of an apparition hanging in the bell tower have been reported, which many know to be the distraught worker. It is said a person can sometimes hear faint sounds of bells ringing and gasps of last breaths being taken in the bell tower on a quiet night when the conditions are just right. Other reports of children crying and laughing have been said to emanate from the abandoned building.

The structure was purchased and intended to become a bed and breakfast, but the owners converted it back to a private residential home and did not open the business as originally planned. Today it stands along the outskirts of Guthrie and although fixed up, still gives passersby goose bumps and uneasy feelings.

Muskogee, Oklahoma

Just 40 miles out of Tulsa is a little town known as Muskogee. The history of the community is just as fascinating as it is problematic. In 1805, Pres. Thomas Jefferson mentioned the little town to the United States Congress. Before the Louisiana Purchase, French fur traders set up small villages and President Jefferson thought it to be in the best interest of the United States to set up a trading post there. These temporary villages caused the launch of that first trading post, but it was not until 1817 that the first settlement was made on the south bank of the Verdigris River.

In 1830, the federal government ordered the removal of the Five Civilized Tribes. In what became known as the Trail of Tears, the Indians were uprooted from their homes and sent into Indian Territory. Many of those people who made, and survived, the trip found themselves in Muskogee.

This old Indian boarding school, pictured in the 1800s, was in Muskogee, Oklahoma.

In 1889, the United States federal court opened in Indian Territory and established itself in Muskogee, Oklahoma. Prior to that, the federal court located in Fort Smith, Arkansas, had jurisdiction over the area. For the first time, a court had jurisdiction over Indian Territory that was located within its boundaries. With the opening of the court along came the land runs, and the area was open to white settlers.

A United States prison was located in Muskogee on the west side of what is now North Third Street. It began in 1898, and that area has seen a lot of strange and disturbing activity ever since. Inside the prison's wooden fence, an area for executions was set up in the courtyard. A scaffold and a rope would decide the fate of all criminals. And it would not be long until the scaffold and rope were put to use. In fact, a second rope was added as the first hanging in Muskogee was a double execution. It was a very hot day on July 1, 1898, when Charles Perkins and K. B. Brooks were condemned to hang. Charles Perkins was sentenced for the murder of George Miller. It seems both men had affections for a young woman named Nancy Adkins. When Perkins went to Adkin's house on December 2, 1897, he was startled to find Miller there with her. The two men argued over who was best for her and as the argument escalated, it ended in gunfire. Charles Perkins shot and murdered Miller in the front yard of Adkins's home. The second man who was to die by hanging that day was K. B. Brooks. Brooks assaulted and nearly killed a young girl in October 1897. Brooks had been hired by a man named Solomon Combs to do farming work. When Combs had to leave for Kansas on a business trip, he left his three daughters in Brooks's care. The girls, who were between the ages of five and 16, saw Brooks as family and trusted him completely. Then, one evening in October, Brooks entered the girls' room and attempted to assault the eldest, Lulu. As she tried to fight him off, her siblings ran outside and hid behind a tree out of view of the assailant. Brooks struck Lulu unconscious and then went to look for the other two girls. Unable to find them, he gave up and returned to the house to find a dazed and confused Lulu stumbling out into the front yard. It was said he assaulted her some more, striking her three times and nearly killing her. Lulu did survive and Brooks was caught after he fled to a nearby farm a few miles down the road. The farmer noticed blood on his hands, sent out the word, and authorities soon picked up Brooks for the nearly deadly attack on Lulu Combs.

Charles Perkins and K. B. Brooks were the first to hang in Muskogee. A double hanging would set a precedent representing the consequence for committing violent crime. It was shortly after the federal court was established that the second, but technically third, hanging would occur. A man named Cyrus Brown was accused of murdering Daniel Cutbert, an elderly local fisherman. Brown was a vagrant who was homeless, hungry, and sick. Cutbert took in Brown and gave him food, shelter, and clothing while allowing him time to heal from his illness. In return, Brown murdered Cutbert and stole his houseboat and other property, but not before tying rocks to his feet and dumping Cutbert's lifeless body into the Arkansas River.

Muskogee also saw tragedy in the form of devastating fires in 1899 and 1909. The Great Fire of 1899 saw the end of Muskogee's downtown district. It was around 5:00 a.m. on a very cold February 23 when a worker at a local plant poured kerosene over coals to build a fire due to the temperatures near zero. When the fuel was ignited, it immediately caused a great explosion, and soon the area was engulfed in flames and billowing black smoke. A citizen began shooting his firearm into the air to act as a warning bell to those residents still asleep. Soon the train whistles chimed in as well and the racket caused many townspeople to run into the street. What they saw was total devastation. Building after building was burning to the ground, and very little could be done about it. The horse-drawn fire wagon had a handheld pump that despite the best efforts of the fireman could not get enough water through the hose to help contain the blaze. Instead, the entire downtown area was engulfed in flames, and the city of Muskogee would have to start over.

It happened again in 1909, when another fire took in the downtown area of Muskogee. On January 14, a fire broke out on Third Street, close to the location where the old prison once stood. It was a cold Wednesday morning when a cook at the Saratoga restaurant was preparing to get breakfast made for his hungry patrons. Unbeknownst to the cook, a gas line had broken, and when he went to start a gasoline engine there was a huge explosion. A fire broke out and spread to several two- and three-story buildings along Third Street, which was soon up in flames. Firemen thought they had come up with a better plan after the Great Fire of 1899, but while the system would have worked better, tremendous population growth in Muskogee had resulted in excess water usage that depleted the water pressure, thus not leaving enough for the firemen to control the fire at the Saratoga. The conflagration soon spread out of control after the pump on the fire wagon also broke. All people could do was sit back and watch the town burn just as it had 10 years before, almost to the day. Half of the buildings on the block at Broadway and Okmulgee Avenues and Third and Fourth Streets were lost to the fire. Once again, it was time to rebuilt Muskogee.

Of course, the city did rebuild and began to start anew, but it seemed as though Muskogee has seen its fair share of hardship and destruction. The cost of the damages exceeded $250,000 from the 1909 fire and Muskogee clearly lost to the raging inferno. Luckily for the citizens of Muskogee, they came out stronger and more determined than ever to be sure that the fire of 1909 did not get the better of them. The little railroad town continued to see growth, but it seems the past was also still crowding it. Muskogee has several documented stories of ghostly sightings, and with its wild history, it makes sense that the past is still haunting the present in Muskogee.

Bacone College

Originally known as Indian University in Tahlequah, this school was established in 1880 and was Oklahoma's first college. In 1885 the Muscogee-Creek Nation donated land, and the school relocated from Tahlequah to its current location in Muskogee. The founder, Indian missionary Prof. Almon C. Bacone, was the only faculty when the school started with just three students. Within a very short time, the school saw tremendous growth and more faculty had to be added to accommodate the expanding number of students. Almon C. Bacone had a vision of providing a Christian education for all Indians, and he was quite successful with his goal. The school was renamed Bacone College in 1910 in honor of its founder.

John D. Rockefeller donated $10,000 to the school and Rockefeller Hall was born. The three-story building acted not only as a classroom building and dormitory but also housed a chapel, teacher's quarters, and a dining hall. The administration area was also located in Rockefeller Hall, or as it was affectionately known, The Rock. The building was taken down in 1938, but some of its materials were used in the construction of Memorial Chapel that now stands in its place.

Public education was mounting from 1918 to 1941, and then president Benjamin D. Weeks needed a way to boost enrollment. He advertised the school as exclusively for Indians and hired Indians for staff. A result of his efforts was paintings that came from students of traditional Indian culture. Those paintings caught the eye of art historians, and the school earned accreditations from various associations.

Today, Bacone College is a four-year liberal arts college offering associate and bachelor degrees in 29 different academic programs. That is not, however, the only thing that Bacone is known for. This old college is also known for its old ghosts. Spectral sightings of Native Americans have been seen walking around campus for generations. Many students report seeing apparitions, hearing strange sounds, and encountering unexplainable cold spots. Complaints of objects being moved when no one is looking are quite common on the grounds of Bacone College. For years people have also told of the phantom riders, an Indian war party that rides through the campus. Witnesses say they can hear the rumbling of horse hooves and the cries of Indians calling out in the night.

On the west side of the property stands a stone pulpit that marks the spot where founder Almon C. Bacone and other missionaries knelt in prayer. It was there they officially dedicated the 160 acres given to them from the Creek Indians to Christian education for American Indians. Rumors that Native Americans are seen at the pulpit have been varied but consistent, but many think the real cause for the haunted school is due to its cemetery. The cemetery at the site is a burial place for Almon C. Bacone and Benjamin D. Weeks along with others associated with the school over its more than 130 years of existence.

Slide projectors set and ready for class have been found empty with the slides thrown about the floor when the classroom has been empty. People driving by have claimed to see an older woman and a man standing in the upstairs window when no one should have been inside. A teacher at the school had a very strange experience. He was in his office next to the classroom grading papers. He realized the class next door was being very loud so he went to see what was going on. When he opened the door to the classroom the lights were off and no one was in there. He could not explain or account for the ruckus he heard coming from the room. One time, the teacher's daughter was with him, and she asked about all the noise next door, so he told her to go check the class. She did, and after finding the same results begged to go home immediately.

Many claim there is a ghost on the third floor of McCoy Hall, a girls' dormitory, and the rumor is a girl haunts the building due to strange, unexplainable activity. The museum on the campus has also told of very strange phenomena as well. The kachina dolls the museum sells are set up neatly lined in a case facing the glass. At certain times, staff has come in to find the dolls scattered about, facing sideways, and in disarray. Could it be Professor Bacone is still keeping an eye on his college? It seems likely that he and other missionaries are roaming the campus and keeping the students in line.

Thomas-Foreman Historic Home

Grant Foreman and his wife, Carolyn Thomas-Foreman, built their house in 1898. Located on Okmulgee Avenue in Muskogee, the family employed a caretaker named Presley. He worked at the home until his death in 1989. Carolyn Foreman died inside the home in 1968, and Presley would tell stories about how he would see Mrs. Foreman watching him from the doorway long after her death. Presley, it seems, has not left either. Sightings of an elderly man doing yard work have been reported at the old home. The house is said to have some intermittent cold spots and to give people a very distinct feeling of being watched.

Tea Room

The old Tea Room is long gone but its ghost is not. Reports of a man roaming around the old historic building were plentiful when it was still around—and so was he. Now the spot is the site of a fast food restaurant, where workers say they are too busy to notice a ghost. Or could it be that when the house was torn down, he went with it?

TULSA'S HAUNTED MEMORIES

Old Sally Brown School

The renovated Sally Brown School is now the site of a bank, but its operations as a school date back to the period 1899 to 1966. It is not just the rumors of a man still lingering that haunt the building, it's the ghosts who actually do. For decades the residents of Muskogee have been telling the story of a man who was brutally murdered here. The legend has been passed down for generations and in the process has been lost in translation. Supposedly there are a few ghosts at the old Sally Brown School but no one knows who they are or what tragedy happened to them to keep them behind. However, sightings are frequent enough to make people stop and wonder about who they are. Likewise, no one knows the identity or purpose of the brutally murdered man who is said to be the resident ghost. So much of this story has been a mystery to the residents of Muskogee, which makes the building and story that much more intriguing. It seems the man is destined to forever remain a mystery.

Green Hill Cemetery

Authorities determined that 380 bodies had to be moved from an old graveyard to make way for a new city park. Green Hill Cemetery in the northwest part of Muskogee is said to be haunted. Considering the discoveries made with the relocation of bodies leaves no guesswork as to why some believe that.

When they were unearthed, 53 of the graves that were to be moved had nothing in them and had to be filled back in. In the graves that did contain bodies, decomposition had left mostly skeletal remains, which were placed in ten-by-ten pine boxes and hauled off to Green Hill and reburied. Some rather startling unearthing, however, took place that day. The contractors hired to do the job came across two metallic coffins in the old burial grounds. One of those coffins belonged to Myron P. Roberts, who died in 1925. Roberts was the newspaperman who started the *Indian Journal*, Indian Territory's first newspaper. When the workers removed the cover casing from the coffin they found Roberts's body totally preserved. Hair combed, clothes neatly pressed, and beard trimmed, like he was just buried that day. Unsure as to why no decomposition had occurred, they buried him again in Green Hill. Another grave they unearthed was of a woman who was apparently buried alive. She was face down as if she was moving around in an attempt to get out. Her arm was across her back and the grave was unmarked. No one knows who the poor woman was or what happened to her. Other graves revealed a body buried with a leather strap around the neck secured with a ring and padlock, and an Indian wrapped in a red blanket that still held the shape of his body. It's quite uncertain what happened to some of those buried in Green Hill, but there are no doubts that a few of them took the secret of what happened to them to their grave.

Labadie Mansion — Bartlesville, Oklahoma

The Labadie Mansion was a 19th-century Victorian home belonging to Frank and Samantha Labadie. It was located about 10 miles out of town, perched upon a large hill deep in the woods. The history of the Labadie family is just as tragic as the haunting that occurs there.

The story begins sometime in the mid to late 1800s, when shortly after Frank and Samantha were married, they began to try to start a family. After years of trying to get pregnant with no success, the couple determined they would not be able to have children. Devastated and heartbroken by the prospect, they had to learn to cope, but Frank seemed to be especially damaged by the notion of never being a father. The couple had a black slave living with them named Enos Parsons. A very loyal man, he did not want freedom after the Civil War and chose to remain with the Labadies. In the winter of 1892, when Enos Parsons was 46 years old, he and Samantha had an affair, which ended with her becoming pregnant. The following spring, Samantha's growing belly could no longer hide her secret. Frank was overjoyed that she was finally able to get pregnant, not knowing the child was not his.

When the child was born in the fall of 1893 it was obvious that the baby did not belong to Frank due to the color of its skin. This sent Frank into a wild rage. He confronted Parsons, who admitted to having an affair with his wife, returned to the home and got his .44 Henry rifle, and headed straight back to Parson's living quarters. Frank shot him once, killing him. Frank then took the body and dumped it into a creek were it was said to sink instead of float. When he returned to the house, he took the baby out of Samantha's arms and told her that he would be sending the baby down the creek as well.

In the spring of 1935, Frank began to go crazy, claiming the ghost of Enos Parsons tormented him. On April 1, 1935, Frank took out his Colt pistol and shot Samantha four times, killing her, and then turned the gun on himself and ended his life with one shot. When the bodies were found and evidence gathered it was noticed there was one bullet missing from the gun, and the .44 Henry rifle was never recovered.

Strange activity and pure evil are claimed to emanate from the property. It is believed that Frank, Samantha, Enos, and the baby still haunt the land where the mansion once stood. After the murder-suicide, the house sat vacant for many years, then suffered two devastating fires. All that remains are the rock walls and foundation amongst some deep vegetation and miles of nothing but lonely woods.

Anyone who dares to venture into the deep woods and visit the empty lot of the former Labadie mansion claims a very aggressive and angry spirit is there, and many believe it is Frank. They tell how something haunts the woods and the even the creek where Enos's body was dumped. Sights of apparitions, feelings of being watched, electronic malfunctions, and disembodied voices calling visitors' name are some of the frightening tales this property calls its own.

Visitors to the property have said they have seen Enos Parsons wandering the woods and creek holding the gun that was used to kill him. Sounds of gunfire are said to be heard there as well, which causes birds to strangely hover overhead. Legends say that a person who looks into the creek can sometimes catch a glimpse of the Labadie baby in the reflection, and an eerie set of eyes will watch people in the woods. Multiple stories of unusual activity and ghostly apparitions have originated from this creepy piece of land over the years. Some truly frightening accounts claim that as a person leaves, he can smell the horrible stench of burning flesh just before the barren fireplace starts to blaze on its own. These accounts have sent people running for safety and vowing never to return to what was once the home of the Labadies.

Tahlequah, Oklahoma

The city of Tahlequah was the final stop at the end of the Trail of Tears, and it is one of Oklahoma's oldest towns. Some very significant history is tied to this land from when the Cherokees were sent to the area. Stories say that the Cherokee tribal government sent two men to locate a site for their new capital. When the two men came to a hillside with two natural springs flowing from it they exclaimed "Tah-le" (two) and "Ah-le-quah" (enough). When men with the tribal government went to see the land the searchers had found, they discovered it was abundant with gifts of nature in its scenery of springs, hills, and forests. Without question the land became the place where the Cherokee established their capital.

They located a large oak tree and used it as council grounds for meetings until a two-story building could be constructed to house the legislative bodies that the Cherokees formed. Shortly after, the nation began deliberating on the laws, punishments, and other tribal precepts they were generating. Many early residents reported the tree was used as the site to grant gifts and awards as well as a place for whippings, hangings, and other severe sentences for those who violated Cherokee law. This tree was a very important facet of the Cherokee Nation and still stands in the middle of town.

Tahlequah was becoming a very large village and saw exceptional growth in the 1830s. When the United States government began moving Indians of the Five Civilized Tribes to Oklahoma, many found their way to Tahlequah and stayed. It was in 1835 when the Cherokee Nation entered into a treaty with the United States. Land allotments began, and the tribal government would soon be dissolved. It was said that even before the treaties were finalized, many early settlers moved from Tahlequah and went across the Mississippi River to find land far away from the white man. They simply wanted to live by their own laws, customs, and time-honored traditions without fear.

Northeastern State University

While the history of Tahlequah is very significant to the Cherokee Nation, it also seems significant to current residents who claim the past inhabitants are still around. One of the most famous hauntings in Oklahoma is the one at Northeastern State University at Tahlequah. Originally the Cherokee Women's Seminary, the school was taken over by the state and made into a university.

When it was a seminary, there was a dormitory mother named Florence Wilson. Wilson was the longtime principal of the Cherokee Women's Seminary. Some say she still haunts Seminary Hall, which was once the site of the girl's dormitory. There have been numerous sightings of Florence Wilson wandering the hallways of Seminary and Wilson Halls in her signature black dress.

Another ghost at Northeastern State is that of a former janitor named Floyd. Legend says that when Floyd was working on the elevator, he fell into the shaft and plunged to his death. Rumors that he haunts the second and fifth floors are common. One student recalls living in Ross Hall for over a year and having some very weird things occur. The student said it was not unusual to come home to her room and find the posters taken off the wall and neatly laid across her bed. She would call Floyd by name and ask aloud that he not remove her posters. Each time the incident stopped for a while, but it would not be long before Floyd was up to his old tricks. When he was not taking posters off the wall, he would move around canned goods while the student was trying to sleep, waking her. Students today claim the ghosts of Floyd and Florence Wilson are still causing a commotion on the campus.

Old Central Elementary School

Many claim children haunt the basement of the Central. The site used to be a Baptist Mission School in the late 1800s. The school was year-round, and the students only returned home for the summer. Those children who died during the winter months were buried in a cemetery on the property. There is also a grave on the north side of the school, which is said to be the child of a family who once resided there. Reports say that children's laughter, crying, and playing can be heard when no children are in the building.

Sequoyah Elementary School

Central is not the only elementary school in Tahlequah to have a ghost. The playground of the old school was once a graveyard. Not just any graveyard, in fact, but Tahlequah's first cemetery. When the old building that had stood there since 1906 was torn down, bones were discovered. Not knowing what to do with them, construction workers threw them into the cement foundation.

Many knew there was a possibility of finding more bones, because just like what happened in Tulsa, the bodies were said to have been exhumed and carefully placed in a lot close by. Unfortunately, not all the bodies got moved, and it appears that those who still roam are not too happy about what happened.

The moving of burial grounds was frequent in Oklahoma, and it is quite a strange prospect to wonder what remains are in the dirt just below any spot. There is a former cemetery across the street from Sequoyah High School in Tahlequah as well. Across the street from the school today are storage buildings, but at one time the bodies of people who died at a tribal insane asylum as well as the elderly, disabled, and orphaned from other institutions were buried there. As these bodies were said to have been exhumed and reburied elsewhere, there are claims that the property is haunted by restless spirits who had their graves invaded.

No Head Hollow

There is a stretch of land along the Illinois River that has a very sad story attached to it. The area is named Goat's Bluff, but its reputation has given it the nickname of No Head Hollow. Legend claims that the widow of a Confederate soldier, in denial of her husband's death, paced the area for days in search of her husband. While she was wandering the land and hoping for his return, she was brutally and violently attacked and killed. The assailants who killed her cut off her head, and it bounced down the bluff below and into the Illinois River. The bluff is said to be haunted, and sightings of the woman have been reported. It seems the lonely widow is still searching for her beloved who did not return from the war.

Stillwater, Oklahoma

This quaint college town 64 miles west of Tulsa has a few haunted tales to tell. The settlement was founded in 1884, when Capt. William L. Couch led a group of settlers, also known as Boomers, to the area. Boomers, as they were called, could have been sent to boost the population. Those early settlers thought property that had yet to be allotted was public domain, and they would squat on the land for homestead until the United States army forcibly removed them. When the group came across a stream, they settled there in dugouts, tents, and small shacks. They named the stream Still Water and felt it could provide necessary water for the few settlers. As more and more people arrived at the stream, it became apparent it would not be able to accommodate everyone, so wells were dug to find more water. The name Stillwater lived on.

Official settlers were those who arrived in the land run of 1889. As they made their way to Stillwater, the Boomers were forced out and back to Kansas. A post office was established and land was donated by Robert Lowry, David Husband, and Sanford Duncan to meet the requirements for having a town. The town was completed as schools, churches, pool halls, banks, grocers, and other businesses starting popping up around the town that would later be known as home to Oklahoma State University. A land grant to make this town a college site was enacted, and Stillwater was born.

Alpha Gamma Rho Fraternity House

This fraternity house on Washington Street in Stillwater is said to be haunted by three former pledges. In 1977, the three young men were working on a castle that was to go on a homecoming float when the scaffolding gave way underneath them. Fraternity pledges Merle, Kevin, and Randall fell into a power line, which electrocuted and killed them instantly.

The house is known to have strange sounds, misplaced items, lights going on and off, and faucets that turn on on their own. The many strange occurrences that have happened in the house make it undeniable to current pledges that three past ones are still there. Different housemothers have been said to witness some strange activity, and one's nephew witnessed an incident as well. The woman and young man were spending the night at the house while getting it ready for the next school year. According to the two, it got so intense they packed up and left early the next morning.

Student Union Hotel and Conference Center

In the Student Union and Conference Center, many strange occurrences have taken place that left students in awe, disbelief, and a bit shaken. Reports of lights turning on by themselves and doors that lock and unlock with no explanation have been numerous. Shadowy apparitions have been witnessed accompanied by cold breezes, glowing lights, and the unmistakable feeling of being watched or followed.

It seems Oklahoma colleges have a few haunted tales to tell, all of which cannot be found in the library's history books.

Spiro Mounds — Spiro, Oklahoma

There is a lot of mystery surrounding Spiro Mounds in LeFlore County. Spiro Mounds is located in Eastern Oklahoma, and is one of the most important archaeological sites in the United States.

The old Indian burial mounds were leased out to two treasure hunters in the 1930s, which gave the site national attention when the men found artifacts after setting off a charge of black powder

151

in one of the largest mounds. The men began to sell the artifacts to collectors all over the world. When their lease was up, they were forced out of the area, and the University of Oklahoma led workers on a controlled excavation of the property to hopefully preserve and salvage what artifacts were left. Among some of the more rare and interesting finds was a smoking pipe referred to as The Smoker. The pipe measures over a foot long and is believed to have been made in the 1100s. Several pipes were found, and archaeologists believe they were brought to Spiro as part of trade and exchange agreements between chiefdoms in smoking ceremonies. Another pipe that was found is referred to as the Lucifer Pipe, due to its creepy design of a man kneeling. Strange or not, it seems the craftsmen of these amazing pipes were way ahead of their time.

Many people, even today, wonder what happened to the first residents of Spiro Mounds. From 750 A.D. to 1450 A.D., this land was believed to have served as important ceremonial grounds for Indians, and evidence gathered from archaeologists demonstrates this fact. Finds show a highly advanced culture in which village craftsmen produced fine pottery, textiles, copper and other metal goods, and sculptures. The area was part of a network of extensive trade routes. For some unknown reason, in 1450 it seems the townspeople simply vanished, leaving everything behind. The site was abandoned, with only a few religious leaders left to perform sacred ceremonies; but eventually they, too, deserted the site.

One of the mounds is a burial mound that includes the remains of Spiro's past powerful leaders. It has been suggested that the largest mound, known as Brown Mound, was the site where great Spiro leaders carried out vigorous, extensive, and complex rituals on the land.

Today, Spiro Mounds is a park where visitors can catch a glimpse of the past and stand along old Indian burial grounds.

Fort Gibson, Oklahoma

Fort Gibson was a military post established in 1824, but many of the soldiers knew it as a place for certain death. The post was created in an attempt to keep peace with the Indians and was referred to as the Graveyard of the Army. Due to its location along the Arkansas and Neosho Rivers, the fort was plagued by disease, and mosquitoes spread malaria. Many soldiers were stationed at the fort, and many of them died there as well. Soldiers stationed at Fort Gibson knew they would have regular drunken poker games to relieve the uneasiness and help them forget about all the lives being lost at this post.

In 1857, the United States abandoned the fort, and the land was given to the Cherokee Nation. During the Civil War, federal troops were temporarily stationed there, and it seems that all the emotion and trepidation still linger at the old fort.

In January 1870, a guard was making his regular patrol of the grounds around Fort Gibson. It was a very wintry day when he discovered the body of a young trooper from the fort known as

Private Thomas. The body was lying across a grave in the cemetery at the fort and appeared to have frozen to death. They took the body to the infirmary and during the autopsy it was discovered that Private Thomas was a female. She had enlisted a few weeks before and passed herself off as a man. The commanding officers and doctors were puzzled and amazed that she managed to get into the army at all. An old priest of the fort came forward to tell a story that is considered one of the most bizarre in American military history. It seems Private Thomas had visited the priest just a few days before her death revealing her secret to him, which was the beginning of the legend of Vivia.

The story of Vivia Thomas has been told and passed down by the people in eastern Oklahoma for generations. Vivia was the daughter of a very wealthy family out of Boston, Massachusetts. Being of such high society, she attended the most prestigious schools and went to the most elaborate social functions and parties. Just after the Civil War, while attending one of these high-class affairs, she met and fell in love with a handsome army officer. They had a courtship of several months before announcing their engagement and wedding plans. Just before their wedding day, the young officer vanished, leaving his brokenhearted fiancee a note proclaiming his need to seek adventure out West, giving apologies, and begging for her forgiveness. Feeling betrayed, Vivia sobbed uncontrollably for days, and then the hurt and embarrassment caused her to leave home to seek revenge.

Viva learned that her former fiance was stationed at Fort Gibson, in Indian Territory, and so she began an adventure of her own. It was a hard, long trip to Fort Gibson but her fiery disposition and need for revenge got her through it. Her journey lasted several months and in her misery and bitterness, she cut off all her long, flowing brown hair. Traveling through the rough parts of the country, Vivia dressed in men's clothing with the intention of protecting herself. Her motive then changed as she realized that she could easily pass herself off as a man. Heading toward Fort Gibson, Vivia was going to enlist in the army at Fort Gibson to be close to her young officer.

She somehow avoided getting caught and stayed clear of her former lover, watching him closely and planning her revenge carefully. Her former beau had gotten together with a young Indian woman who lived near Fort Gibson, and he visited her frequently. Vivia would follow him through the darkened woods and get more and more angry with each step. She could no longer bear to see him with anyone else, and her plan for retribution was about to come into fruition. It was a bitter cold winter night in December of 1869 when Vivia followed the young officer to his lover's house with her rifle in tow. She waited for him behind a large rock and when he rode by on his horse she shot him in the chest and he fell off his horse. She left him there, and the next day his lifeless body was found by someone passing by. The soldiers and officers at the fort assumed he had been killed by Indians and buried him in a cemetery near the fort.

Proud of herself for getting revenge, she was satisfied and at first felt justified in her actions.

As the days went on, however, she realized the magnitude of what she had done; her guilt soon overcame her, and she was deeply grieved. Every night, she would visit the cemetery and grave where the young man was buried and weep hysterically while praying for forgiveness. She would spend hours at the site trying to repent for her sin of murder. One cold evening as she was visiting his grave and as hypothermia set in, she got sleepy and lay across his gravesite. That night, she froze to death and was found the next morning. Many believe that her spirit still roams and haunts the national cemetery.

For decades, reports of a young soldier pacing about and weeping loudly have come from the fort. Many people know it to be the ghost of Pvt. Vivia Thomas, who is still looking for peace. When the commanding officer figured out the story of Private Thomas, he erected a stone in the Circle of Honor among the soldiers who had died during their service. Her stone seems a bit out of place. It simply reads, "Vivia Thomas, January 7, 1870."

Tulsa Area Lakes — The Studio at Grand Lake

Grand Lake, like many other areas near water, was widely known as an assembly area for Native Americans. They would gather to practice rituals, ceremonies, and other celebrations. It was said at night their fires danced in the river's reflection and the chanting and stomping of powwows echoed in the distance. But with settlement comes death, and burial grounds were built close or inside the villages. Those areas are now long gone, built up and over or dug out, leaving no remembrance of the men who first came to the region.

Leon Russell, a famous musician, built a house on this land and has some firsthand stories himself and from other musicians that seem to say the fallen predecessors are still among us and seek the recognition that was so harshly taken away from them. On Russell's former property, there were three houses near the lake and a recording studio perched upon a hill behind them. Big iron gates protected the estate from intruders but could not keep out the ghostly presence. There have been some very famous people who have recorded or visited the studio including Bob Dylan, Bob Segar, J. J. Cale, the Gap Band, and many others between 1972 and 1974. It was a rock-and-roll haven for those who wanted to play music all night and sleep all day. In 1974, after another full night of recording, a former sound engineer and his wife took a nap on the third floor of the home. The couple woke up to find a small fire teasing a pile of clothes and flickering very close to them, looking as if it would catch them on fire, which it did not. The small glimmers would suddenly and quickly go out but two hours later returned to a different pile of clothes on the floor just at the foot of their bed. Spontaneous small fires were said to have happened a few times, and there were several witnesses to the events.

Some former employees claim there was a malevolent spirit that resided in the basement of Russell's former home. A recording studio was set up in the basement, but few musicians ever wanted to record there. Several complained of becoming nauseated as well as having a sense of impending doom come over them. The heaviness of the air around them made people leave rather quickly. On three different occasions, an apparition of a translucent Native American has been witnessed walking through the control room. It was said that when a band was full of energy and excitement as they prepared and rehearsed for road tours is when the phantom would be seen. It seemed the band's enthusiasm stirred up sightings of the apparition, who is apparently a fan of Leon Russell's music. Some even claim there is a photograph of the Native American floating around somewhere to prove the house did have a resident ghost.

Rumors claim that when the house was being built for Leon Russell, he asked the contractor about the land and its history. The man told him that according to records, the lot contained an Indian burial ground but he did not know exactly where.

While the spirits of the past loved Russell's music, they did not take so kindly to other visitors. Many talented musicians graced the studios of Leon Russell, and it was said if the spirits disliked someone, they were downright unfriendly. In fact, rumors say the spirits had a special aversion to the legendary Bob Seger, and he had a few experiences while recording that he found to be quite unpleasant. One evening, during a recording session, the sound engineer was in his room when the musicians plowed through his door shaken, nervous, and excited, telling him, "There's something awful happening to us in this house!" The engineer went to see what was going on, and when he walked into the studio he described it as ice-cold energy and very loud sounds of chains rattling. He claimed that it got really intense when all the doors started slamming shut right in front of the group.

The very large and very heavy gates on the property are said to have a mind of their own or are manipulated by the spirits at the Lake Studio. The non-electric gates at the time were said to have been viewed swinging open by themselves to welcome some visitors and closing and locking rather abruptly when trying to keep someone from leaving.

The house is now owned by a Tulsa chiropractor, and while he has yet to experience anything, his family members have laid claim to the hauntings that take place there. In fact, his wife refuses to go to the house alone and believes it to be haunted. Whoever the mysterious Indian man is, it seems he misses the late night jam sessions and the creative outlet it became for visitors to the home.

Tulsa's Haunted Memories

Lake Tenkiller

Rumors of a killer octopus are said to have derived from the sightings of a large underwater carnivore roaming the freshwater Lake Tenkiller. This body of water has had an unusually high number of deaths from drowning, and many contribute it to the mysterious sea creature. Native American legends have been brought down from generation to generation about the large monster in the lake that eats men alive. They say the animal is about the size of a horse. Indians often chronicled tales of a creature with tentacles in the lakes and rivers surrounding Tulsa.

Oklahoma also had its very own version of a Loch Ness Monster. A 27-foot vertebra was found in central Oklahoma that archeologists say belonged to a marine sea creature that once made its home in prehistoric lakes and rivers. It seems the water around Oklahoma has been inhabited by legendary creatures for centuries. Large ripples, countless drownings, and other factors make a few visitors to area lakes watchful of the water for what may be considered Oklahoma's lake monsters.

Oklahoma POW Camps

While it may seem a little hard to believe, between the years 1942 and 1945, there were places called *Nazilager* (Nazi camps) located all over Oklahoma. Many of the old prisoner-of-war camps are said to be haunted, and much of it can be contributed to the murders and other insane activity that went on there. It was said to be so bad the camps gained reputations of being like Devil's Island or Alcatraz and were even nicknamed as such on occasion.

It was rumored that prisoners were bullied, cajoled, and threatened into complying with the hardcore fascist movement by their fellow captives. For instance, one of the Wehrmach prisoners was a man with no political affiliation whatsoever but an offhand comment about Hitler ended up costing him his life. His head was beaten relentlessly with a baseball bat by another prisoner who was an unwavering Nazi. Late at night, the camps were a frightening place to be. So much so that American military police were quite reluctant to go inside. The camps had much less supervision, if any, on the insides as they did on the outside. It was said at times the prisoners were permitted to patrol themselves, and that is when it got ugly. In the late hours, the cries, moans, and pleas of those who dared to go against Nazi propaganda could be heard. Nazi loyalists were fanatical in their devotion to the cause and felt determined to make others feel the same way.

These old camps are long gone, but there were several that were not known to most people. Several "private" camps were also located in and around Tulsa. Lack of knowledge about their locations makes people wonder just where they could have been and leaves no doubt as to why Oklahoma is so haunted.

Spirit Lake — Antlers, Oklahoma

While not technically a part of Green Country due to its far southeast location, this quiet little town in the foothills of the Kiamichi Mountains cannot be left out. The name of the town derives from the numerous deer antlers left behind by Indian hunters in its heavily wooded wilderness. The land around Antlers was once a part of the Choctaw Nation prior to statehood in 1907 and is just a two-hour drive from Tulsa into the southeast portion of the state. Surrounded by crystal clear lakes, outlaw caves, beautiful mountains, and cascading waterfalls, this area was once a secluded hideout for outlaws like Jesse James, the Daltons, Belle Starr, and many others. While this little town has not changed much from the days of outlaws and bootlegging, the lakes it is known for are also its biggest curse.

The bewilderment that shadows the town is a captivating tale of its nearly 200 years of haunted history. Deep in the woods along a hill in the crest of the mountains is a place known as Spirit Lake. Today the locals refer to it as Lost Mountain Tribe. Anyone who has lived in the area for any length of time will agree the land is extremely haunted and one that nobody would want to intentionally visit. Spirit Lake sits in the midst of a clearing in the high mountain wilderness. In the 1800s, a woman was murdered and drowned in the lake, and thus the lake got its name. According to the story, the woman still haunts the lake and is seen bending down at the embankment but vanishes just as she makes eye contact with an onlooker. Another account recalls a young girl who was murdered and thrown in the lake by outlaws who were seen fleeing the site on horseback at a very fast speed. While many residents do not wish to talk about it, it seems there have been an excessive number of deaths in the area, making it extremely haunted. Stories of witches burned at the stake around Spirit Lake date back as far as anyone can remember. Sightings of ghostly apparitions have been said to scare off locals and visitors from wandering into the vicinity. In fact, locals say that while riding their horses along a trail near Spirit Lake, the horses will refuse to go near the area, forcing them to turn around and therefore never explore the entire trail.

In 1905, the land surrounding Spirit Lake was known to be the site of a cult that lasted for nearly 15 years. A father and son who claimed they were God and Jesus found themselves with 25 to 35 followers, mostly women. They were known to steal from ranchers and the father-son team would often have sexual relations with the females in the cult. This activity led to many birth defects and children who were drowned in the lake out of fear of their being possessed by the devil due to their deformities. Nearly all the children were drowned at Spirit Lake. Sometime between 1918 and 1920, the cult abandoned the area and left everything behind. No one was found, but all of the cultists' personal property, buildings, food, and clothing were left as if they were coming back, but they never did. No wildlife could be found in the area either.

A few years later, a commune took over the area for a short time and tried to make a secluded living there, but it was said the area was so haunted, strange forces would run out anyone who dared to spend the night. Thinking the haunting was a result of the ritualistic sacrifices made by the cult, they fled the site, again leaving it abandoned.

The Antlers County courthouse, which contained all the records of the unusual happenings at Spirit Lake, burned down in 1930. According to the records clerk at the sheriff's office, the land had a lot of problems with the people who would try to occupy it. Complaints of people going crazy, fleeing the area with crazy stories, and obviously being spooked by something were common for many years, and the land was left abandoned and uninhabited.

The city of Antlers is a thriving small community today, but anyone who stops and talks to old-timers finds them reluctant to discuss what happened in their town many years ago. Spirit Lake has also been called Lost Lake due to the number of people who have attempted to settle there only to abandon it later. Many people today stay away from the site in fear of awakening the spirits that apparently still linger in the clearing. If the adventurous try and find the site, they will not get much help from locals, either. Many of them try and ignore that the area exists and are much less likely to help find it in fear of spiritual repercussions. The area of Spirit Lake will forever be a mystery.

AFTERWORD

The history of Oklahoma and its painful past is but a small clue into why the land is haunted. Indian traditions are rich in spirituality and methodology, and many believe that the land is both blessed and cursed. This idea leaves behind so many questions and so many possibilities that a person cannot help but question what spirits remain behind to tell of a time that once was.

Make no mistake, Tulsa is referred to as America's Most Beautiful City for a reason. The economy, scenery, and hospitable citizens make Tulsa and its suburbs an amazing place to call home. The horrific history Tulsa once faced is forever engraved in its culture, but a modern visitor to the city would not know it. Tulsa citizens are some of the most thoughtful, kind, and caring that you will ever find. Today Tulsa is a thriving community known for its historic buildings, trendy districts, and insatiable ability to make anyone feel at home despite where they are from. The days of drunken cowboys terrorizing neighborhoods are long gone, but the history that molded this community gives it character and definition.

No matter how beautiful the city or how friendly the citizens, every piece of land has a story to tell. And if the sod and the trees could talk, their words would leave most of us in awe and disbelief.

www.arcadiapublishing.com

Discover books about the town where you grew up, the cities where your friends and families live, the town where your parents met, or even that retirement spot you've been dreaming about. Our Web site provides history lovers with exclusive deals, advanced notification about new titles, e-mail alerts of author events, and much more.

MADE IN THE USA

Arcadia Publishing, the leading local history publisher in the United States, is committed to making history accessible and meaningful through publishing books that celebrate and preserve the heritage of America's people and places. Consistent with our mission to preserve history on a local level, this book was printed in South Carolina on American-made paper and manufactured entirely in the United States.

This book carries the accredited Forest Stewardship Council (FSC) label and is printed on 100 percent FSC-certified paper. Products carrying the FSC label are independently certified to assure consumers that they come from forests that are managed to meet the social, economic, and ecological needs of present and future generations.

FSC
Mixed Sources
Product group from well-managed forests and other controlled sources

Cert no. SW-COC-001530
www.fsc.org
© 1996 Forest Stewardship Council

Find Your Place in History.